MW01235619

AMERICA
WILL
BE
SAVED!

Carl Becker

XULON PRESS

Xulon Press

2301 Lucien Way #415

Maitland, FL 32751

407.339.4217

www.xulonpress.com

XULON PRESS

All Scripture quotations are from the *King James Version*, public domain, or are derived from that translation. The author has capitalized pronouns that refer to God.

All poems have been written by the author. The poem "Real Freedom" references four freedoms, named by President Franklin Delano Roosevelt in his State of the Union Address, 1941: "The Four Freedoms Speech." The poem "America! America!" is inspired by the poem "America the Beautiful" by Katherine Lee Bates, 1894, 1911.

Printed in the United States of America

ISBN – 13:978-1-6322-1081-4

Ebook – 978-1-6322-1082-4

To contact the author: carlbecker316@yahoo.com

Dedication

To my Pastor,
Mirek Hufton,
Senior Pastor
of World Harvest Church, Roswell, GA,
a shining example
of what every Pastor in America should be!

Check out our multi-cultural church at:

whcga.com

In Loving Memory

Of a great hero of faith, apostle and evangelist,
Reinhard Bonnke (1940-2019),
who passionately proclaimed the prophecy:
<u>America will be saved!</u>
Bonnke wrote:
"America is clearly a land in need of the preached gospel ...
They say that America no longer cares
to hear the gospel preached—
that a nationwide revival in this jaded land is impossible.
But I say to them that
GOD SPECIALIZES
IN TURNING IMPOSSIBLITIES
INTO POSSIBILITIES.
This harvest is not only possible, it is likely.
For people of faith, the time to believe is NOW,
before it is seen and everyone climbs on the bandwagon ...
Bible prophecy is history written in advance.
That is how exact and correct it is. It is unalterable.
God will fulfill His Word, to the dot on the last i.
WE MUST LAY HOLD OF IT AND STAKE OUR VERY LIFE ON IT ...
Did God say, America will be saved? Did He?
Oh, yes, He did.
And He means what He says,
because He always says what He means.
GOD HAS NOT GIVEN UP ON AMERICA ...
Let's trust God, and the Lord, who raises the dead
and sets prisoners free, will do what He has promised."[1]

---

[1] Reinhard Bonnke, *Raised from the Dead: The Miracle That Brings Promise to America*, Whitaker House, New Kensington, PA, 2014. pp. 161-168 (emphasis mine)

Table of Contents

JESUS IS LORD!

Where the Spirit of the Lord is, there is freedom:

not freedom to sin
not freedom to murder babies or anyone
not freedom to be as perverse as we please
not freedom to abuse power.

NO!

Where the Spirit of the Lord is, there is freedom:

freedom from the guilt and power of sin
freedom from tyrannical government
freedom from fear of death
freedom from lack.

Where the Spirit of the Lord is, there is liberty:[2]

liberty to live for God
liberty to worship, pray to and obey God
liberty to proclaim the Gospel of God
liberty to love, lift and help others.

The Spirit of the Lord is in me and on me,
and by the Spirit of the Lord I declare the decree:

AMERICA WILL BE SAVED!

America is the land of the free and the home of the brave,
a liberty-loving, Bible-obeying
Constitutional Republic under God
with opportunity, freedom and equal justice for all!

---

[2] 2 Corinthians 3:17

Introduction

Have you figured out what is going on? *We are in a battle today for America's identity, destiny and future.* This battle is a nasty battle—it is a battle of ideas, principles and governing ideologies—and *you* must be armed for battle: not just with guns, but more importantly, with Truth. You must not be uninformed, uninvolved or unnerved. Nations, like people, can stagnate, decline or continually change for the better. How America changes is up to you and me.

What I need you to understand and appreciate is that the *First* Amendment is the basis of the *Second*—and every other freedom and right that we Americans treasure. The freedom to worship the one true living God and to preach the Gospel of the Lord Jesus Christ is *the essential ingredient* that makes America, America.

America is supposed to be the land of the free and the home of the brave. America was founded on faith in God, for the glory of God. America is about freedom *under* God—not about freedom *from* God. America is about freedom from coercive, controlling and crippling government. *That* is the heart of the spiritual battle raging today.

Please—do not "tune me out" if you are not "into God." God is into you! God is a good God, and He wants good things for you and for America. Let your defenses down as you read, *please,* and you will be immeasurably blessed. [Maybe you should read chapter 12, first.]

Perhaps, you ask, "Can't we leave God out of politics?" I ask you: Is it wise to compartmentalize our Creator? In order to get our politics right, our heart must be right. *Spiritual* freedom is the foundation of *political* freedom. Our faith in God ought to impact our politics, and if it doesn't, we're not thinking right. The objective here is to produce intelligent, liberty-loving, virtuous *Americans* who will use their God-given rights to change the course of history.

Introduction

I am an American writing for all Americans. What is said in this book transcends party politics and ought to govern every political party, every politician and everyone who cherishes America. Every American must make a fresh commitment to independent, but Bible-based, thinking.

The battle for America's identity, destiny and future began in 1620 when the Pilgrims came to America with a freedom vision and with an impassioned vision to spread the love and the Gospel of Jesus Christ. The battle for America's soul has raged ever since. Make no mistake: there are those who want America, as America, to die—and to be replaced with an atheistic Marxist state. I say: *Not on my watch!*

In one sense, the battle over America's soul will not be over until Jesus sets up His kingdom on earth. Every two years in the United States, we have an election that decides all 435 seats of the House of Representatives and every four years we have a Presidential election. No one election will win the battle forever. But, one election can set us on the wrong path. Elections have enormous consequences. What this means, for those of us who love America, is that we can never relax. If we win one election, we must not coast; if we lose one or more than one, we cannot panic, quit and hide in sorrow. *If the devil is in war mode, we dare not be in drift mode.*

What is going on today? The devil is working feverishly to create a new world order, but America and freedom-loving Christians are in the way. The devil wants to control everything and everyone through the mark of the beast. Those who hate God will use any means to gain power, "win" elections, take your guns, and seize all your liberties (and they'll never give them back). Those who want the government to dictate what we can think, say and do are driven by demonic spirits, and they must be stopped. They *will* be stopped by those who live by the Truth. Atheistic socialism is the anti-American, hellish path to tyranny. **Atheistic-socialism will kill our freedoms, our finances, our families, our faith, and our future.**

Young people: social media and college campuses are battle grounds, and you will be hosed, relentlessly, with untruths. You will be told that Christianity is merely one *theory* of life. *It is not!* Christianity is God-made reality. *Christianity is a life-giving relationship with the living God through Jesus Christ by the power of the Holy Spirit.* You will be told that Christians are anti-science. This is a lie. Our God made the laws of science! We are against pseudo-science that denies the reality of the living God, the Master Designer of our universe. Science and medicine must be anchored in Scripture, tied to freedom and ruled by law—or they will be weaponized by tyrants. Remember, all scientists are not in lock-step; moreover, there is in many scientists and doctors egregious bias against God. Fearlessly question scientists, doctors, professors, politicians, self-appointed experts, and *especially* today's master manipulators: the media. One aim of this book is to empower you to spurn to seduction of secular socialism, to prepare you to recognize, resist and refute the lies, half-truths and smear of our antichrist culture. Get ready to think, rethink, and then change the world.

We must all learn to think God's thoughts after Him. Why? The death of intelligence causes the death of freedom. How do we know God's thoughts? We read His Word: The Bible. When you esteem the Bible as God's Word, the Holy Spirit will make it alive to you, a burning fire in your heart. Hope will come alive in your heart, hope for a future worth living, hope for America to stay free and to fulfill its destiny.

Every American needs to understand that our *Declaration of Independence* rests on God's Declaration, on the Bible. Why does this matter? Because freedom is the fruit of the tree of liberty, and that tree is planted in the hearts of those who know the Truth. The Bible is inspired by God; it is God-breathed. It is God's personal declaration of who He is and what He has done and how He works.

To declare means more than to spout off. A Declaration is a forceful statement of Truth from which there is no retreat. You never "walk back" a Declaration; rather, you stand on it fearlessly, regardless of the personal sacrifice it requires of you. You stand your ground to make it your reality, no matter how fierce or well-funded the opposing forces are that would make it an ephemeral bubble.

The *Declaration of Independence* is the preeminent American document. It is a rejection of government overreach, which it refers to as "usurpation." It would never have been written had England's king not made himself into a tyrant and tried to impose unreasonable and arbitrary law on the thirteen colonies. But the living God can make good come out of evil. Therefore, I do not despair.

The *Declaration of Independence* is our American gospel. Gospel means, good news of great joy to all people.

Atheistic-socialism is a pseudo-gospel. It is a fake and a fraud, and nations that are deceived by it lose their freedom. Think Cuba. And Venezuela. And China.

The future of America depends on our understanding of and respect for both true gospels, the Bible and the *Declaration of Independence*. Read the *Declaration* in the light of all the government overreach that has been going on since the curse of COVID-19 upended our lives. Meditate on each sentence enumerating the grievances of the American colonists, so that the spirit of liberty will live strong in you. When you finish, read God's Gospel, the Bible. Then, God will use you to preserve freedom to future generations.

Perhaps no one person embodied what America was at its beginning more than George Washington, our nation's first President, an American with *uncommon sense* and *uncommon faith*.

There is a beautiful portrait of Washington with head bowed, kneeling in prayer in the snow, beside his horse.[3] The painting records a true incident. At the time, Washington was serving as commander-in-chief of the American Army during the Revolutionary War. He and his army were encamped at Valley Forge, northwest of Philadelphia, from December of 1777 to the spring of 1778. Washington was not posing for an artist; this was no publicity stunt. As far as Washington was concerned, he was praying in secret; he certainly wasn't praying for show. A Quaker just happened to witness him praying, and heard him asking the God of heaven's armies to intervene because at stake was the cause, not just of the country, but of the world. Why was he on his knees? Because he felt, deep in his soul, that America was worth fighting for, that America was worth saving. He knew that he needed God's help or else the war would be lost. He knew that God would stay on his side, if he stayed on God's side. He knew that if he forsook God, then God would forsake him. He believed that there is a just and almighty God who judges nations according to their piety, virtue and intelligence. He believed that if he humbled himself *under* the mighty hand of God and reaffirmed that though he was commander-in-chief, he was under the command and authority of God Most High, then he could claim the protection and help of God. Bottom line: George Washington believed that if he prayed, then *America would be saved*. This bitterly cold winter was, perhaps, the low point of the Revolutionary War, but it became the war's turning point because Washington fell on his knees in earnest prayer.

Americans!

America is an uncommon nation, a nation worth saving!

This book is not about America's demise and death. It is about America's rebirth and resurrection.

---

[3] The painting is by Arnold Friberg

Uncommon sense understands that America is about freedom *under God*, not about being forced to do whatever the government arbitrarily decides.

Uncommon vision sees the chilling fact that today's atheistic elite have their own arbitrary absolutes which they contrive out of their reprobate sin-poisoned minds, which they intend to impose by force on all society, on you and on your children.

Uncommon discernment perceives that when we come under the authority of the Lord Jesus Christ, He puts us in authority over the devil, demons, and those who would turn our nation into a socialistic dystopia.

Uncommon backbone resolutely refuses to bow before any human-god or unconstitutional edicts.

Uncommon love chooses life for all the unborn.

Uncommon compassion desires mercy for every sinner.

Uncommon faith boldly declares: *America will be saved!*

The United States of America belongs to the Lord Jesus Christ. Our nation is His. I reiterate: one election should not cause us to over-celebrate, nor should one election send us into a tailspin. We need a long-term strategy to be the dominant influence in every level of government, in every grade of education, in every aspect of our culture. What we desperately need today is Great Awakening. And that is what we will have! We are not helpless or hopeless. We have faith in God, for whom nothing is impossible. But for America to be saved from authoritarian government, you and I must be saved from our sin, because sin is the worst tyrant. Thank God there is a living, Savior who gladly gives us freedom from sin and His own risen life. His name?

JESUS!

1

HOUSE DIVIDED

**Jesus said, "Every kingdom divided against itself
is brought to desolation; and every city or
HOUSE DIVIDED against itself shall not stand."[4]**

Jesus speaks absolute Truth in a world rife with lies. Absolute Truth is Truth you cannot change. You may not like the Truth. You may try to ignore it. You may vociferously and vehemently argue against it. You may ridicule, scorn or even literally fight against any who speak it. You may connive and conspire to smother it and suppress it. But none of that changes Truth. After you are tired out, the Truth still stands. After you die, the Truth still stands. The absolute Truth is: If the house is divided, it is going to fall. Jesus said so, and Jesus cannot lie. Jesus always speaks Truth in love. Every nation is a house. If our American House is divided against itself, it cannot stand. We have been divided before; we are now divided again.

The year was 1858. A hopelessly polarized nation was about to attack itself.

---

[4] Matthew 12:25

The horrible Civil War was two years away; the *Emancipation Proclamation*, five years away. Abraham Lincoln, then running for the Senate, gave a pivotal address on the subject of slavery, which was the cause of our American House then being divided. Lincoln knew why the nation was headed for catastrophe.

"We are now far into the fifth year, since a policy was initiated, with the avowed object, and confident promise, of putting an end to slavery agitation. Under the operation of that policy, that agitation has not only, not ceased, but has constantly augmented ... it will not cease, until a crisis shall have been reached, and passed. 'A house divided against itself cannot stand.' I believe this government cannot endure, permanently half slave and half free. I do not expect the Union to be dissolved—I do not expect the house to fall—but I do expect it will cease to be divided. It will become all one thing, or all the other."[5]

Lincoln's deep respect for the wisdom of Jesus sharpened his own powers of perception. Lincoln knew that Jesus was no liar. He knew that Jesus—above all others—could be trusted. He knew that Jesus had revealed unalterable spiritual law: *Any nation or house divided will not stand.* Our American House, under the leadership of President Lincoln, became a free house for ALL. Yes, it took over 100 years for the scourge of racism to be slapped back—but the dye had been cast in 1865. Slavery was gone, never to return. America was not a slave nation. America was the land of the free—for everybody. The *Declaration of Independence* was the seed for that happy outcome.

It is now the decade of the 2020s, and we need to see with 20/20 vision.

Our American House is divided deeply again.

That means that great change is here: for better or worse.

2

---

[5] Abraham Lincoln, Cooper Union Speech, February 27, 1860.

Like a thousand tornadoes, atheism, moral relativism and licentiousness have ripped across America, leaving a trail of tears from coast to coast: incalculable anguish and agony, innumerable families shredded by infidelity, drugs, alcohol, violence, crime and 'no-fault' divorce. The suicide rate among teenagers is an alarming sign that something is terribly amiss. What is wrong?

We are divided: not black against white—though some would divide us along those lines, not north against south, not even Democrat against Republican ... and not rich against poor: though some would divide us along those lines.

We are divided like this:

God

against

non-God

What do *you* want America to be?

A nation *with* God or a nation *without* God?

A nation *under* God or a nation *against* God?

Consider carefully. Choose wisely.

Any nation that defies, dishonors, disobeys and deletes God is going in only one direction: *down.*

Today we are in a spiritual struggle for America's soul.

We are also in an intense battle for *your* soul.

You are not a bystander. *Your* future is on the line.

Today we must choose between the American Dream of liberty and justice for all and the nightmare of atheistic socialism imposed on us by authoritarian government. We are in a vitriolic and vicious war of incompatible ideologies with clear consequences. If the insanity and irrationality of atheistic socialism wins, then truth, liberty, morality and prosperity all die. We must wake up now, or else. Every American must choose between honoring the living God as God, and the folly of exalting self or government as god.

What is *your* choice?

Think seriously and deeply about America's identity and destiny *under God*. These are not trivial matters: they go the heart of America's future. All three—America's *identity*, America's *destiny*, and America's *future*—are under attack.

America's *identity* is: one nation *under God*.

America's *destiny* is: the land of the free and the home of the brave, where every American citizen freely enjoys their God-given rights to life, liberty and the pursuit of happiness.

America's *future* is: the greatest nation on earth *under God,* shining forth the hope of what is possible for every nation.

Sadly, there are those who hate God, who hate America. They do not want God to exist. They do not want freedom to exist. And, if you disagree with them, they do not want *you* to exist, either. They do not just want a nation *without* God; they want a nation *against* God, militantly against the moral authority of God. They want a nation in which *they* are god. They want the Church sidelined, silenced and shut down. To them, the Church of the Lord Jesus Christ is not just a non-essential nuisance to be tolerated, but a toxic hindrance that must be eliminated. *Believers, beware!* Open your eyes, before it is too late!

The following two diagrams summarize our choices.

In the first, the Lord Jesus Christ is at the center. You will notice that four wonderful, priceless national treasures flow from His Lordship. In this model, government is limited in power, and its purpose is to protect our freedom, promote Truth and morality, and incentivize prosperity for all.

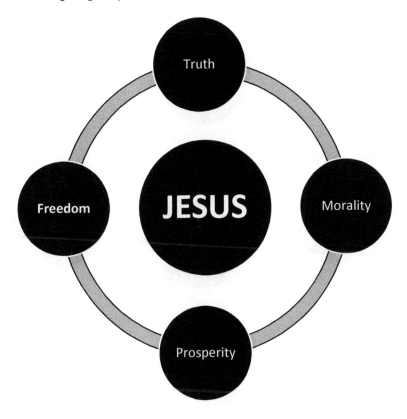

This model portrays what America is and must always be.

In the second diagram, Jesus is gone, and the atheistic government has become god in His place. But what is the result? The four blessings are also gone, and unmitigated horror reigns instead. Instead of protecting our freedoms, now the government confiscates our money, mandates controls in every sphere of our life and harshly penalizes us for non-compliance—all because we supposedly can't take care of ourselves.

Be sure: this model is the *antithesis* of America. It is the *undoing* of America. It is the *enemy* of America.

Atheists want to remake America into a secular socialist nation; they want to undo America's DNA, and fundamentally and irrevocably alter our national identity and destiny. All that will wreck our future!

UNDER GOD: OUR ONLY SAFETY

This is what I know: **It is better to be *under God* than to be under the fist of ruthless atheistic tyrants.** It is better to trust the promises of the God who cannot lie than to trust the empty promises of politicians who love to lie. It is better to obey God wholeheartedly than to be a powerless pawn of over-reaching, hyper-controlling government. It is better to be under the moral law of God than to indulge in unchecked immorality. As for me, I choose to be *under God*. This phrase, *under God*, lies at the heart of our nation's identity, destiny and future.

What does it mean, to be *under God?* Consider this: children are *under* their parents. What does that mean? They are under the authority of their parents, and their moral duty is to honor and obey their parents. For a nation to be *under God* means that we honor and obey God, esteeming Him as He is: our Maker and Father. We never "out-grow" God or declare our independence from God. We are forever His children—not baby children— but always His children. We can and should grow, spiritually, and become His mature sons and daughters and His partners, but that will never happen if we in laughable arrogance imagine that we are His equal. He is the Eternal One; we are not. He is our Creator; we are not. A tough pill, for some, to swallow.

Abraham Lincoln closed his 1863 Gettysburg Address, a magnificent and monumental Address, with these words:

*"that this nation, **under God**, shall have a new birth of freedom."*

President Lincoln was an intelligent, self-educated man; while he did not invent the phrase *under God*, neither did he insert it into his address just to fill air. Perhaps, in spare moments, he read the dictionary ... which dictionary? A few years earlier, in 1828, Noah Webster published his *American Dictionary of the English Language*, in which we have this remarkable (but politically incorrect) entry: "UNDER, In subordination to. ***Under God, this is our only safety***."[6] Whether Lincoln read this definition or not, he knew that every nation would either be a nation *under God* or a nation *without God*, and that if his nation unwisely chose to be *without God*, then it would be *without freedom*.

Perhaps Lincoln read this from Josiah Quincy, American orator of freedom, in 1774:

> *"Blandishments* [flatteries] *will not fascinate us, nor will threats of a 'halter' intimidate. For, **under God**, we are determined that wheresoever, whensoever, or howsoever we shall be called to make our exit, we will die free men."*

Or this, from General George Washington, in his Orders to the Continental Army, given on July 2, 1776:

> *"The fate of unborn millions will now depend, **under God**, on the courage and conduct of this army."*

Or this, from Samuel Adams, the Father of the American Revolution, in 1780:

---

[6] Noah Webster, *An American Dictionary of the English Language*, S. Converse, New York, 1828, reprinted by The Foundation for American Christian Education, San Francisco, CA. 1967, 1995.

*"May every citizen in the army and in the country, have a proper sense of the Deity upon his mind, and an impression of that declaration recorded in the Bible, 'Him that honoreth Me I will honor, but he that despiseth Me shall be lightly esteemed.' The people must, **under God**, give energy to this all-important call, and enable the combined Forces at once to put an end to the War."*[7]

Lincoln realized that the phrase, *under GOD,* not only assumed the existence of God, but affirmed the interaction of God in our lives. *UNDER God* meant that we are not God's Judge, but that He is our Judge; and that we can only enjoy God's providence and blessing if we willingly come under His moral authority and acknowledge His sovereignty. Lincoln was a diligent Bible-reader. In his Bible, Lincoln read:

"Humble yourselves UNDER the mighty hand of God, that He may exalt you in due time."[8]

Lincoln knew this verse (and quoted it in one of his proclamations):

"Blessed is the nation whose God is the LORD."[9]

Lincoln knew this verse:

---

[7] William J. Federer, *AMERICA'S GOD AND COUNTRY, Encyclopedia of Quotations,* AMERICSEARCH, INC., St. Louis, MO, 2000, p. 524, 639. The Adams quote is dated June 12, 1780, in the *Original Writings of Samuel Adams,* by Samuel Adams, Volume 4.

[8] 1 Peter 5:6

[9] Psalm 33:12 President Lincoln, in a Proclamation March 30, 1863, wrote: "it is the duty of nations as well as of men, to own their dependence upon the overruling power of God, to confess their sins and transgressions, in humble sorrow, yet with assured hope that genuine repentance will lead to mercy and pardon; and to recognize the sublime truth, announced in the Holy Scriptures and proven by all history, that **those nations only are blessed whose God is the Lord.**"

"Righteousness exalts a nation; but sin is a reproach to any people."[10]

These statements are *absolutes*. They always apply to any nation anywhere at any time. They cannot be changed. We cannot fight against them and succeed. They reveal reality. *Righteousness exalts a nation:* Right living in the sight of God makes a nation exceptional. When *"We, the People"* live virtuously by grace and boldly legislate virtue, we become a nation that God blesses and prospers. *Sin is a reproach:* Debauchery brings disaster—personally and nationally.

Wake up, Americans! Tyranny is at our door. Atheistic political correctness will escort it in, to our sorrow. Wise up, Americans! The freedom to be immoral is a lovely illusion that leads straight to hell. Freedom divorced from God's authority is the fantasy of fools. Fools without *uncommon sense* think that God's version of right and wrong is oppressive and stupid. Surely, we are not a nation of *fools!*

WHY ARE WE DIVIDED?

Why was the nation divided back in 1858? The answer: many had departed from the *Declaration of Independence* and its bold proclamation that all men are created equal. They wanted freedom only for themselves, but not for all. They demanded the freedom to enslave others. Perverse freedom!

Why are we divided today? The answer: many have departed from the *Declaration of Independence* and its bold proclamation that we are endowed by our Creator with certain inalienable rights. They disdain the very thought of a Creator and have mysteriously, miraculously evolved into being god themselves. Strong delusion!

10

---

[10] Proverbs 14:34

Either God is God, or mere mortals are god. There can be no compromise between these core convictions. Either the *Declaration* will prevail, or atheistic evolution will prevail.

Atheistic evolution is an attack on the soul of America.

Atheistic evolution is unscientific. Now, that will ignite the ire of atheists! Atheists love to smear Christians as being anti-science. But our God made the universe and its laws. Our God made gravity. It is a lie that science and Scripture are opposed. *Atheistic* science—science that denies the existence of God our Creator—is opposed to Scripture, but real science is not. To assert that there is no Creator and that we evolved from nothing by chance over millions of years—is unscientific and unintelligent, and is *the irrational religion of atheism!*

What gave birth to American exceptionalism? Not atheism. Not self as god. Not *self*-reliance. Not reliance on government. Rather: Reliance on God, reverence for God and right living in the sight of God! Without these qualities, our exceptionalism and our liberties will wither.

An illustration is in order. Picture a huge tree with great branches, a tree so large that untold numbers of birds enjoy its shade, decade after decade. That tree symbolizes America. We could call it the Tree of Liberty. Millions have enjoyed the shade of this tree, decade after decade. But now there are those who, though having enjoyed the shade of the tree, would kill it by pouring poison on its roots, on the roots of faith in God, on the roots of Biblical morality, on the roots of Biblical Truth! What happens when a tree has been poisoned? It begins to die! America, a glorious Tree of Liberty, has sustained awful damage from atheistic poison. But it is not time to cut the tree down. It is time to bring life to our roots once again!

America's identity, destiny and future are all on the line—and *you* have a say in all three. *Your* say is pivotal.

America is not just about freedom any more than a cake is just about sugar. **America is about freedom *under God*.**

May I remind you of our nation's *Pledge of Allegiance?*

I pledge allegiance to the Flag of the United States of America,
and to the Republic for which it stands,
*one Nation **UNDER GOD**,*
indivisible, with liberty and justice for all.

Who is God? *"For the LORD is our Judge, the LORD is our Lawgiver, the LORD is our King; He will save us."*[11] In all three relations, God is over us. God Almighty is not only our Creator: He is the Supreme Law-giver, whose moral absolutes produce wholeness and freedom without self-destruction.

Scripture reveals God as He is. The true God loves people so much and hates tyranny so much, He created the first free nation. Remember Exodus? Remember Pharaoh? Remember the Red Sea? God delivered an oppressed people from the chains of Egyptian bondage. *This God is the God of America!*

By the grace of God, I will *never* surrender
America's identity, destiny or future *under God*
to the pseudo-intellectualism of reprobate atheists!

Why? I see more clearly than atheists. I see that when a nation becomes a godless nation, then fraud, abuse of power, misuse of public funds, and lying become the new normal, bringing about the death of freedom. I see farther than atheists. I see the awful end of their agenda: poverty and tyranny. I see where atheists are headed: *backwards* to a hopeless era in which stone-cold agents of the atheistic state wield unchecked power against the people.

---

[11] Isaiah 33:22

To demolish America's moral and spiritual foundations is to destroy our national future. Atheistic socialism, therefore, is *the foremost* existential threat to the future of the United States.

There is a God. Man is under God. These undeniable realities are the solid foundation of the United States. *America* and *God* are inseparable. America is one nation *under God*. This is America's precious *identity*.

There is no god. Man is God. These lethal lies are the undoing of any civilization. They are the core of Communism and socialism, and were the sandy foundation of that evil empire—the Union of Soviet SOCIALIST Republics.

There is a God. Or: *There is no god.* These statements are irreconcilable and produce ethical systems that are incompatible. *Man is under God.* Or: *Man is God.* These statements likewise are contradictory—and they cause outcomes as radically different as heaven and hell.

The two ethical systems can be simply portrayed like this:

<u>GOD</u>

<u>Man</u>   or: **<u>Government</u>**

<u>Government</u>   **<u>Man</u>**

In the God-model, Man—representing all people—is *under* God but *over* the government. This model, which flows from the stream of Scripture and which is enshrined in our *Declaration of Independence*, produces maximum liberty, opportunity and prosperity. In the atheistic model, God is gone, and Man is on the bottom—under the fist of authoritarian government, with no God to rescue him. This undeniably inferior model is "sold" to us by atheists through this lying presentation:

13

Man

Government

When God is gone, lies reign. Pause and ponder.

Being God is very heady stuff. If you are God, then you are the King of the universe, you get to make the laws of the universe, and you get to determine right and wrong. Wow!

What really happens when we choose to be God? *A stunning inversion!* When we foolishly eliminate God, instead of becoming God ourselves, *government* becomes God. When government becomes God, people become slaves of the State—a heartless State that has no regard for the life, liberty, prosperity or rights of its subjects. What is the truth?

 # 1 - <u>YOU</u> ARE <u>NOT</u> GOD.
 # 2 - <u>GOVERNMENT</u> IS <u>NOT</u> GOD.

History proves that whenever government becomes God, all hell breaks loose. *Cruel compassion, arbitrary absolutes, cold-blooded coercion*: these are the bitter fruit of the ethical system pushed by today's atheistic elite. Let every American know: self and State are pernicious fake gods, and they produce death, slavery to government and misery for all!

America's House is divided between two diametrically opposed ethical systems: the Christian and the atheistic.

We must choose sides. I must be blunt.

- *Atheism is the opium of fools.*
- *Christianity is the fountain of life.*
- *Atheism leaves the heart stone cold.*
- *Christianity is living fire.*

To the atheist, Christianity is inherently homophobic and Christians are bigots and hate-mongers who must be silenced. *These are lies from the devil's warped mind.* To the atheist, the Bible is irrelevant literature, the basis of Puritanical oppression. *These are lies from the devil's depraved brain.*

The Bible is the true Source of our political liberty. President Andrew Jackson declared to an impudent infidel: *"That Book, sir, is the Rock on which our Republic rests."*[12] The Bible is not theory; *the Bible is Truth.* The Bible is not literature; *the Bible is Life.* The Bible is not the word of man; *the Bible is the Word of God.* I repeat: The Bible is Truth—absolute, authoritative, anointed Truth. The Bible is universal, ultimate, uplifting Truth: and Truth gives birth to freedom. *The future of the United States of America depends squarely on how we esteem the Bible.*

If America becomes a nation *without* God, then government will be *on* the people, *over* the people and *against* the people, the exact opposite of what President Lincoln envisioned: *"government of the people, by the people, for the people."*

If America becomes, in its schools and colleges, an atheistic nation that shuns and silences Christians, then gone will be the dream of Dr. Martin Luther King, Jr. of a table of brotherhood where racism is a thing of the past—and in its place will be a nightmare of violence, poverty and perversion.

Do you really think that America can be great if we war *against* God, if we censor the Bible, if we eliminate the Ten Commandments and substitute for them the fluid immorality of God-haters? *"If we ever forget that we're one nation **under God**, then we will be a nation gone under."* President Reagan said that, and he was right.[13]

---

[12] See Henry Halley, *Halley's Bible Handbook*, Zondervan Publishing House, Grand Rapids, MI, 1962, p.19. Halley wrote: "The Bible is the most precious possession of the human race."
[13] President Ronald Reagan, August 1984 Prayer Breakfast speech

I warn you: Today's atheistic elite (whether they are in a shadow government behind the scenes or in elected office) have the same goal as the Chinese communists. They aim to amass all power in their hands and strip you of all freedoms. They will use any crisis—real or manufactured—as a pretext that necessitates their "compassionate" power-grab, so they can ensure your safety and security. They want a subservient population that they can control, that does what they're told without hesitation, that believes what they're told without questioning, that has no power to protest, and that is dependent on the largess of the State for their very survival. If that angers you, your *uncommon sense* is working! Today's atheistic elite want to be the overlords of a new world order in which Christians, Christianity and Churches are terminated. They boast, in their devilish pride, as Lucifer boasted, *"I will exalt my throne above the stars of God."* As if to say, *"We will run the Church; we will rule the world; we will define the morality of the New World Order."* But He who sits in the heavens laughs at them in derision and pronounces against them the judgment He pronounced against Lucifer: *"Yet thou shalt be brought down to hell, to the darkest dungeons of the pit."*[14] This is why I do not fear atheists with their Luciferian delusions or draconian edicts. *I fear God.*

America is a house divided. Something will change. *How* America changes depends on you and on me. America will either become the cursed land of atheistic-socialism, or it will, by a fresh wind of the Holy Spirit, be a blessed nation *under God,* spreading the life-giving, life-changing Gospel of the Lord Jesus Christ to every nation on this planet. I am not pessimistic or petrified. I am passionate about America's identity, destiny and future *under God!* I release my faith and hope:

America will be saved!

---

[14] Isaiah 14:13-15; see also Psalm 2

2

UNCOMMON SENSE

**"For they are a nation void of *uncommon sense*;
neither is there any understanding in them.
O that they were wise, that they understood this,
that they would consider their latter end!"**[15]

Jesus wept when He saw Jerusalem and exclaimed:
**"O that you had the *uncommon sense*
to know the things that would bring you peace,
but now they are hidden from your eyes."**[16]

Both Moses and Jesus foresaw the future of their beloved nation
and lamented. However, no eternal decree from God doomed Israel
to be conquered by Babylon or by Rome. Israel's stubbornness and
pride deprived them of *uncommon sense* and blinded them to their
deficiency and vulnerability.

What, exactly, is *uncommon sense* and, where does it come
from?

---

[15] Deuteronomy 32:28-29 KJV: "They are a nation void OF COUNSEL" – void of,
lacking, the invaluable counsel of God!
[16] Luke 19:41-42

Uncommon sense comes from God, as does common sense. Eliminate God, and you are left with ... nonsense. *Uncommon sense* is the God-given ability to distinguish truth from misinformation, propaganda and lies. *Uncommon sense* is the God-given ability to discern right from wrong and the genuine from the counterfeit. *Uncommon sense* is the God-given ability to see what ought to be done and how to do it. The humble can have it. The arrogant cannot. Those who fear God have the seed of it. Those who mock God will remain blind, esteeming atheistic delusion as the epitome of wisdom.

Atheistic socialism is national nonsense.

Atheistic socialism takes power away from *"We, the People"* and transfers it into the hands of a self-appointed elite who concoct policies that centralize power in their own hands and that reduce the nation to poverty. Socialism cannot cure poverty: it only metastasizes the curse. "Free" health care, "free" education and "free" food is sweet seduction. *"Free" stuff will cost you all your freedom and all your money!* You are not a poor, powerless, pitiful victim entitled to endless government hand-outs. If you grasp these realities, you have at least a bit of *uncommon sense.*

Samuel Adams proclaimed piercing words in his oration *"On American Independence"*:

> **"Courage, then, my countrymen!** Our contest is not only whether we ourselves shall be free, but whether there shall be left to mankind an asylum on earth, for civil and religious liberty ... If ye love wealth better than liberty, the tranquility of servitude than the animating contest of freedom—go from us in peace. We ask not your counsels or arms. ***Crouch down and lick the hands which feed you.*** May your chains sit lightly upon you, and may posterity forget that ye were our countrymen!"[17]

---

[17] Adam's speech is dated August 1, 1776

If you would rather have the government take care of you from cradle to grave, than be free, then *crouch down and lick the hands that feed you!* You have betrayed the brave Americans who fought and died to make this nation the land of the free.

Free people are not worshippers of Marx. Their eyes have been opened. They see Truth. Free people have been set free by Jesus. They have tasted His goodness, and so, are repulsed by the thought of mere mortals acting like God. *Free people have uncommon sense.*

Free people trust in God, not in the government. Their simple motto is: **IN GOD WE TRUST!** Their mantra is not, "In the World Health Organization I trust; after all, they know what's best for me." *Free people have uncommon sense.*

Free people are rightly suspicious of a government with unlimited powers. Free people have it figured out: the government that takes *care* of you will surely take *control* of you. *Free people have uncommon sense.*

Free people know that a one world super-government is contrary to everything they hold dear; they do not wish to hand over their blood-bought national sovereignty to an international body that has zero loyalty to the United States of America. *Free people have uncommon sense.*

Free people know that it is economic surrender to let an unelected cabal of banking powers dictate the money supply at their whim. *Free people have uncommon sense.*

Free people value freedom *from* the guilt and power of sin. They know that internal spiritual liberty is the all-important foundation of external civil liberty. They know that without freedom from sin, they will be expendable fodder for petty dictators. They know that those who refuse to be governed by God will be ruled by ruthless tyrants. *Free people have uncommon sense.*

Free people like to read. They especially like to read the Bible and to them, conscience-numbing entertainment is inferior to church. Free people like to think. They like to do their own thinking. They don't want to be told what to think and what they can or can't do— especially not by God-hating atheists! Free people know that resistance to tyrants is obedience to God. Frederick Douglass, who experienced the dark night of slavery firsthand, warned, *"To make a contented slave, it is necessary to make a thoughtless one. It is necessary to darken his moral and mental vision, and, as far as possible, to annihilate the power of reason."*[18] Free people take warning, because *free people have uncommon sense.*

Free people like to create wealth. They know that Marxism is a lie, a sham and a fraud. They know that when the government supposedly redistributes wealth, it actually ends up in the hands of the ultra-rich. Free people like to invent, innovate, invest and specialize; they see money as a tool with which they can do great good for others. They don't want their wealth confiscated by selfish hypocrites in the name of saving the planet or reducing the world's population. Why? *Free people have uncommon sense.*

Free people perceive the marred nature of people: that without God, we are all selfish, greedy and untrustworthy. This unpleasant truth means that no government should be given absolute power: there has to be checks and balances along with separation of powers. Free people value limited government. Free people discern: what the government gives, the government can take away; and, the more government expands, the more government demands. Free people get it: the purpose of government is not to provide free stuff, but to protect freedom and God-given rights, and to ensure one system of justice for all. Why? *Free people have uncommon sense.*

---

[18] Frederick Douglass, *Narrative of the Life of Frederick Douglass, an American Slave*, Penguin Books, NY, 1845, 1986, page 135.

Free people like the idea that America is such a beautiful land of liberty that millions want to come here. They do not hate foreigners; they just want them to come legally, obey our laws and uphold America's identity and destiny *under God*. They want secure borders for the same reason they have doors and locks on their homes and businesses. *Free people have uncommon sense.*

Free people like to own property; they like to own their businesses. They chafe against superfluous regulations; they hate being bullied by bureaucrats. They don't like being ordered around and surveilled by an arrogant elite that plays by a different set of rules. *Free people have uncommon sense.*

Free people appreciate Ronald Reagan's humor: *"The trouble with our liberal friends is not that they're ignorant; it's just that they know so much that isn't so."*[19] Free people laugh—but then a wave of sobriety washes over them. They know that government policy based on disinformation and atheistic propaganda will take their beloved nation in one direction: *down. Free people have uncommon sense.*

Free people know that the more atheistic socialism gains power, the more intolerant it becomes. Free people are not deceived. They don't buy atheistic nonsense. Free people want America to stay free and to spread freedom all over the world. They believe that is America's glorious destiny, *under God*. Free people with *uncommon sense* know that being *under God* is better than being under tyranny.

Their unflinching war-cry is, **"Give me liberty, or give me death!"**

Their unabashed motto is: **"Live Free or Die!"**[20]

Free people with *uncommon sense* perceive the identity, the destiny and the future of the United States of America. This is what free people know, and I print it in big letters:

---

[19] Ronald Reagan, *Time for Choosing*, October, 1964. *Magnificent speech!*
[20] Patrick Henry, March 23, 1775; the motto of New Hampshire

America is one nation UNDER GOD.

**America is the land of the free—
not the land of atheistic socialism.**

**America does not need more *government*—
America needs more *GOD*.**

You need *uncommon sense,* but you can't get it from atheists. What they have to give is lethal *nonsense.*

Fulfilling our God-given destiny to spread the light of freedom to every nation will require more than your *uncommon sense.* America will only be saved for its destiny if you add to your *uncommon sense* an *uncommon commitment* to God and His moral laws. Jesus said, *"Take My yoke upon you ... My yoke is easy, and My burden is light."*[21] The yoke of Jesus is His moral authority; His burden is His moral commandments that we obey by His empowering grace. We will either voluntarily come under the gentle yoke of the Lord Jesus Christ, or we will be forced to wear the oppressive yoke of an all-controlling government. To wear no yoke at all, is not an option. To trumpet freedom from God is to choose chains forged by demons who have no mercy. If you comprehend all these realities, you have a high level of *uncommon sense.*

As for me, I take the yoke of Jesus. I have found by experience: His burden is to me what wings are to a bird. And that is no burden at all.

Will you join me? *Uncommon sense* partners with *uncommon faith* and courageously declares:

America will be saved!

---

[21] Matthew 11:29-30

3

Young People, Re-Think!

**"I have more understanding than all my teachers:
for Thy testimonies are my meditation.
I understand more than the ancients,
because I keep Thy precepts."**[22]

Young people: You've got to know more than your godless teachers; you've got to know what they're *not* telling you; you've got to know their bias against the God of the Bible; you've got to know that their heroes: people such as Emerson, Voltaire, Darwin and Marx—were in fact children of the devil who spread darkness and deception like deadly disease; you've got to do your own research and your own thinking; *above all, you've got to encounter the living God for yourself,* experience His love and enter into an everlasting relationship with Him through Jesus Christ.

Today's atheistic elite want to condition and control—not your hair, but your mind. They view fear as a weapon by which they can indoctrinate, manipulate and subjugate you. But that's not your *destiny.* Your *identity* is not determined by them. Your *future* is not for them to make.

---

[22] Psalm 119:99-100

To win in life, to fulfill your destiny *under God,* you've got to have both *uncommon sense* and *uncommon faith.* With *uncommon faith* I see my true identity in Christ: I am a child of God. I am who God says I am. With *uncommon sense* I see our national identity: America is one nation, under God. *The battle for America's identity and destiny is a battle for America's heart and soul. And you cannot escape this battle.*

It's great to be technologically savvy—but it's hazardous to your health to be clueless about American history and the favorite book of our Founding Fathers—the Bible.

It's way too risky to go unarmed onto the battlefield: and that is exactly what social media and college campuses are! To know Truth first-hand is to be armed. Educate yourself, then influence your social media!

Educate yourself, then dare to challenge the sacred presuppositions of God-haters!

Ignorance is the enemy of liberty.

ARE YOU INDOCTRINATED ... OR INTELLIGENT?

There are three levels of learning: (1) indoctrination (2) education and (3) intelligence. Indoctrinated people ignore the Bible. Educated people read the Bible. Intelligent people live by the Bible.

Intelligent people keep thinking after the professor has stopped talking.

Indoctrinated people derisively dismiss God and consequently, buy the lie that the government will take good care of them. You know what that is? *Uncommon delusion!*

It is a platitude that education is the answer to our problems, but *education without God is indoctrination.* Education without God is atheistic propaganda.

Education without God is downright dangerous. Why? When you expel God and the Bible from school and let atheists censor what is taught, you create a mental swamp in which the dangerous ideas of Marxism and socialism and communism and nihilism and materialism breed like virus-carrying mosquitoes.

The first Americans were not merely freedom-lovers. They were God-lovers! They didn't spend hour after hour imbibing the toxic brew of atheism served up by reprobate French philosophers; their favorites were not Aristotle, Plato or Socrates, but Moses, Jesus and Paul. They did not worship the goddess of reason; they spent Sunday after Sunday in church, reading the Bible and having their souls lit by fiery preaching. In church they learned the truths of democracy; in church their morals were formed so they could be free!

An indoctrinated people cannot be mobilized for virtuous action—but they can be duped into thinking that socialism is the answer for all life's problems. *It is not!*

Study 100 years of socialism, from 1919-2019, and you will discover what socialism has produced. Calamity. Carnage. Why?

Socialism is a mirage based on lies.

Socialism is married to atheism. Socialism puts *government* in the place of God, while atheism puts *self* in the place of God. This toxic combination kills freedom, prosperity, America ... and you.

Atheistic-socialism is a covenant with hell. I boldly declare: *America is the sweet land of liberty, not the land of atheistic-socialism!*

If you have been schooled in public schools and public colleges, you have already been inundated with untruths and anti-Christian misinformation. Now it is time for you to *rethink, reexamine* and *rebel against* the group-think of social media that brands Christians as weird, brainless science-haters!

God gave you a mind: refuse to let it be the dumping ground for the misinformation of the misinformed!

Let me warn you: you will get mad when you wake up and realize that your teachers and professors lied to you—and that you paid for it. But when that moment comes, and it will come, use your anger as fuel to change our nation!

Indoctrinated people have been told (in the atheistic schools they attended) that they are "free to learn"—but in English they were assigned only anti-Christian books to read; in civics they were taught a false tale of American history which deliberately deleted the vital role that Christians played in the founding of the United States; in science they were taught the lies of evolution and billions of years, and were not told that leading scientists in every branch of science believed in God. Indoctrinated people don't bother to read the *Declaration of Independence*, the Constitution—or the Bible—and so, they deprive themselves of *uncommon sense*. Indoctrinated people unthinkingly accept propaganda as truth—when it is, in actual fact, blatant *untruth*. Indoctrinated people cannot tell the difference between the madness of Marxism and the sagacity of Solzhenitsyn. Indoctrinated people don't know why Cuba and China have no freedom. Hmmm. Can you spell: a-t-h-e-i-s-t-i-c s-o- c-i-a-l-i-s-m?

Rise up and refuse to be indoctrinated!

Does America have a godly heritage? Yes! Does it matter? Yes! Does it matter that YOU know how America came to be one nation *under God?* Yes! If you know the Truth, you will be empowered to preserve this great nation and its God-given liberties for future generations.

Educated people have read the Bible. You cannot claim to be educated unless you have read the entire Bible—the greatest of all books, the Word of the living God. Please, do not take offense. Take my challenge! Turn the television off and read *The Book*!

If you want to know God first-hand and develop *uncommon sense*, the best place to start is with the Bible.

Intelligent people live by the Bible. They don't just listen to the Bible—they put it into practice. Intelligent people apply the truth of God's Word to their everyday lives.

Intelligent people know that they have been endowed by their Creator with certain unalienable rights; they see clearly why no human person can be trusted with unlimited power; they understand that God has framed moral absolutes that if obeyed will produce lasting happiness; and they humble themselves under God's authority and ask for grace to obey God's moral laws.

Intelligent people know that freedom can only survive when it is based on moral and godly foundations.

Intelligent people know that the first Americans courageously left Europe, not with government subsidies and not to get rich, but to be free to worship God and for the advancement of the Christian faith. The Pilgrims were not relying on government-as-god, but on the living God. The freedom they cherished was freedom to obey God and to spread the kingdom of God. They knew that civil freedom was the direct result of the influence of Christianity, and that, in proportion as real Christianity diminished in power, immoral practices—such as slavery—would gain power.

Wake up, young people! Your pop culture is setting you up to be the willing instrument of your own ruin!

Shakespeare advised: "*To thine own self be true.*"

Dare to question this celebrated sagacity! Don't just quote a saying as if it is true. Re-examine it. Re-think! Make it better! How about this:

To God be true!

"To be or not to be, that is the question." No. Re-think! Make it better!

To be His, or not to be His, that is the question.

Don't commit suicide: commit your soul to Jesus!

What is liberty?

Do not confuse *liberty* with *licentiousness* or *anarchy*.

Licentiousness is freedom from all moral restraint.

Anarchy is the absence of legitimate authority and law. The anarchist bellows: "No one can tell me what to do!"

Moral anarchy is the broad road to hell.

Liberty is the ability to do what God requires without interference or arbitrary penalty from the government.

America is not about freedom from God and the moral law of God.

America is about freedom under God: voluntarily coming under the authority and providence of God.

OUR DECLARATION OF INDEPENDENCE

Our *Declaration of Independence* is a great spiritual document that contains our nation's DNA, and it is the foundation of America.

Our *Declaration of Independence* represents the triumph of faith in God over tyrannical, totalitarian government.

Our *Declaration of Independence* does not rest on the hubris of atheistic enlightenment. It rests on nothing less than Almighty God. It is not a godless dissertation. It is incompatible with atheistic socialism.

Four times—in the first two sentences and in the last two sentences—there are explicit references to the living God.

"When in the Course of human events, it becomes necessary for one people to dissolve the political bands which have connected them with another, and to assume among the powers of the earth, the separate and equal station to which the Laws of Nature and of **Nature's God** entitle them, a decent respect to the opinions of mankind requires that they should declare the causes which impel them to the separation.

"We hold these truths to be self-evident, that all men are created equal, that they are **endowed by their Creator** with certain unalienable Rights, that among these are Life, Liberty and the pursuit of Happiness ...

"We, therefore, the Representatives of the United States of America, in General Congress, Assembled, **appealing to the Supreme Judge of the world** for the rectitude of our intentions, do, in the Name, and by Authority of the good People of these Colonies, solemnly publish and declare, That these United Colonies are, and of Right ought to be Free and Independent States ... And for the support of this Declaration, **with a firm reliance on the protection of divine providence,** we mutually pledge to each other our Lives, our Fortunes and our sacred Honor."

How does our *Declaration of Independence* refer to God?

- **"Nature's God."**
- **"Creator."**
- **"The Supreme Judge of the world."**
- **"Divine Providence."**

Does this sound like an atheistic document to you? It doesn't, to me. Does our *Declaration* sound like a deistic document, as if God is detached? What do you think?

On whom did America's Founding Fathers rely?

On *"Divine Providence."*

So then, their motto was not, "I got this."

Neither did they say, "The government's got this."

God is the Lawgiver, the Ultimate Authority. *"Endowed by their Creator"* means that no mere mortal man can undo what the Eternal Creator has done; no government can override, negate or annul the moral decrees of the Lord God Almighty.

Can't you see what this means for us today, namely, that atheistic socialism morphs our identity into tyranny? Can't you see that atheistic socialism will turn our golden door into a prison door? Can't you see that moral relativism, in the name of inclusion and diversity, leads to the death of morality and the death of Truth? Can't you see that immorality is the counterfeit of love, that anarchy is the counterfeit of liberty?

Uncommon sense sees that our *Declaration of Independence* opened a river of freedom whose source is the Bible. If we abandon faith in the God of the Bible, the great principles enshrined in our *Declaration* will perish.

Uncommon sense sees that we are foolishly polluting that river and poisoning ourselves with the deadly toxins of atheistic philosophy, abortion and homosexual perversion.

Uncommon sense sees that we cannot progress beyond the self-evident truths of our *Declaration*. We can live up to them, but we cannot surpass them.

To reject our Creator and His moral law is not to go forward, but backward. Any civilization that practiced child sacrifice and homosexuality is extinct. Do you want America to be extinct?! I don't. I live here! Anarchists and socialists cannot give you a better future— they can only wreck it.

You will meet people who seem to specialize in attacking Christianity, in mocking the Bible, and in ridiculing what they will label as "archaic" beliefs. Their arguments may temporarily baffle you, but I have learned this: just because someone points out what *they* think is a contradiction in the Bible, does not mean that it actually *is* a contradiction; and, just because *I* can't solve any given dilemma or objection at the moment, does not mean that others, who have trained for years in the field of apologetics, cannot easily and swiftly offer a stunning rebuttal. [Please read this footnote!][23] Truth is never shaken by atheists' rants. Truth can always withstand scrutiny. So, don't let your faith be torpedoed by ridiculous complaints that God-mockers raise. Remember, God's love reaches the heart; His Truth will transform the mind.

We are routinely told that all 'respectable' scientists today are evolutionists. This is a blatant lie, designed to train you to deride and dismiss any scientist who is a creationist. Nevertheless, it is remarkable that the founding scientists of various branches of science were *creationists*. Look at this list:

- Johannes Kepler (1571-1630)—celestial mechanics
- Isaac Newton (1642-1727)—calculus
- Michael Faraday (1791-1867)—electromagnetics
- Louis Pasteur (1822-1895)—bacteriology
- Gregor Mendel (1822-1884)—genetics
- and many more, including: Louis Agassiz, Lord Kelvin, Blaise Pascal, and James Clerk Maxwell.

Many of these pioneers of science were committed Christians. Knowing that puts a pin in the atheists' balloon.[24] Truth is, many brilliant scientists today believe in God and the Bible and the reality that God created the heavens and the earth by His word.

31

---

[23] Check out great Christian apologists: *Josh McDowell, Ravi Zacharias, Francis Schaeffer, D. James Kennedy.* Your PASTOR can help you, too!
[24] See D. James Kennedy, *What If Jesus had Never Been Born.*

Another example. Our National Anthem, the Star-Spangled Banner, has a fourth verse, ending with these words:

"Blest with victory and peace, may the heav'n rescued land
Praise the Power that hath made and preserved us a nation.
Then conquer we must, when our cause it is just,
And this be our motto: 'In God is our trust.'
And the star-spangled banner in triumph shall wave
O'er the land of the free and the home of the brave!"

"Praise the Power" is referring to the Lord God Almighty, who intervened in behalf of the young nation! America is called a land rescued by heaven from tyrannical government! And, don't you love our motto?! Now inscribed on our money. Why weren't you told *all that* in your schools? This fourth verse was the seed for the undoing of tyranny, just as the second sentence of our *Declaration* was the seed for the undoing of slavery.

Francis Scott Key did write a third verse, in which he said that neither the hireling nor the slave were able to help the enemy prevail. *His fourth verse negates his third.*

God is on the side of the oppressed, not on the side of the oppressor. Key was a Christian. Was he imperfect? Yes, he was. We need not throw our National Anthem in the trash basket because Key was dismissive of the efforts of slaves to free themselves by joining with the enemy of our nation; we need to recognize the man's awful flaws; we must resolutely reject the bad in him, but keep the good he produced in spite of his defects.

DEISTS? I DON'T THINK SO

Some argue that the Founding Fathers of America were not Christians; that they were Deists. That is, they believed that God created the world, but then left it, and that God is detached, distant and uninvolved in our lives. How do you answer that?

Start with the Pilgrims who came to America in 1620. They were not slave owners kidnapping and selling slaves. No, they came for a different purpose. They didn't come to eat turkey on Thanksgiving. They had something much higher in mind, something so extraordinary that it became the cornerstone of the United States of America. 102 brave men and women got on board the Mayflower, fleeing religious persecution. After a voyage of over two months, they arrived in Massachusetts and on November 11, 1620, most of the adult men signed the *Mayflower Compact*. It reads as follows:

*"**In the name of God, Amen**. We, whose names are underwritten, the Loyal Subjects of our dread Sovereign Lord King James, **by the Grace of God,** of Great Britain, France, and Ireland, King, Defender of the Faith, etc. **Having undertaken, for the Glory of God, and Advancements of the Christian Faith** and Honor of our King and Country, a voyage to plant the first colony in the Northern parts of Virginia, Do by these Presents, solemnly and mutually, **in the Presence of God** and one another, covenant and combine ourselves together into a civil Body Politic; for our better Ordering and Preservation, and Furtherance of the Ends aforesaid ... **Anno Domini**[25], 1620."*

Why weren't you given *this* to read?

The Pilgrims came to America to be free: not to be free *from* God, but to be free to worship God and to preach the Gospel. They did not risk their lives so they could keep their faith in private, compartmentalized and away out of sight. No! *They came to advance Christianity!* This is the heart of America! This is why, when our Constitution was adopted, a Bill of Rights was quickly added.

33

---

[25] ANNO DOMINI is Latin for "In the year of our Lord" – a blatant and bold reference to none other than our Lord Jesus Christ. Away with "BCE" – an atheistic attempt to rewrite history!

The FIRST Amendment reveals the secret of America:

*"**Congress shall make no law** respecting an establishment of religion, or **prohibiting the free exercise thereof; or abridging the freedom of speech,** or of the press; or the right of the people peaceably to assemble, and to petition the government for a redress of grievances."*

The *first* of all freedoms and the *foundation* of all other freedoms is the freedom to worship God and to proclaim His Good News! *Freedom to worship the one true God is the heart and soul of America!*

Read for yourself the unedited speeches of America's Founding Fathers and you will discover delightful truth: America's most influential Founding Fathers were God-fearing men who aimed to create a moral nation *under God* with liberty and justice for all. Were they imperfect? Yes. Just like you and me. Most were *not* Deists. They knew that God was not absent from His world, but had come to us through Jesus and the Holy Spirit.

How can you know? It's called study; it's called independent research; it's called refusing to accept "dumbed down education" as the "new normal." Question the narrative pushed by those who delete God! Ask yourself why they would hide the truth, twist the facts, or revise the historical record. Where can you find the greatest trove of American history? Investigate the footnote below.[26]Then, instead of reading Marx, read Alexander Solzhenitsyn (1918-2008), who knew the horrors of Marxism first-hand, in the USSR. Teach yourself!

Patrick Henry (1736-1799) gave his passionate oration, *Give Me Liberty or Give Me Death,* in 1775, at a church. He spoke up in behalf of America's independence:

---

[26] JACKPOT! David Barton, a living American historian, has done so much work for you. Check him out at *wallbuilders.com*, especially his book: *Original Intent.*

"No man thinks more highly than I do of the patriotism, as well as abilities, of the very worthy gentlemen who have just addressed the House. But different men often see the same subject in different lights; and, therefore, I hope it will not be thought disrespectful to those gentlemen if, entertaining as I do opinions of a character very opposite to theirs, I shall speak forth my sentiments freely and without reserve. This is no time for ceremony. The question before the House is one of awful moment to this country. For my own part, I consider it as nothing less than a question of freedom or slavery; and in proportion to the magnitude of the subject ought to be the freedom of the debate. It is only in this way that we can hope to arrive at truth, *and fulfill the great responsibility which we hold to God and our country.* Should I keep back my opinions at such a time, through fear of giving offense, I should consider myself as guilty of treason towards my country, and *of an act of disloyalty toward the Majesty of Heaven, which I revere above all earthly kings* ... We have petitioned; we have remonstrated; we have supplicated; we have prostrated ourselves before the throne, and have implored its interposition to arrest the tyrannical hands of the ministry and Parliament. Our petitions have been slighted; our remonstrances have produced additional violence and insult; our supplications have been disregarded; and we have been spurned, with contempt, from the foot of the throne! In vain, after these things, may we indulge the fond hope of peace and reconciliation. There is no longer any room for hope. If we wish to be free-- if we mean to preserve inviolate those inestimable privileges for which we have been so long contending--if we mean not basely to abandon the noble struggle in which we have been so long engaged, and which we have pledged ourselves never to abandon until the glorious object of our contest shall be obtained--we must fight! I repeat it, sir, we must fight! *An appeal to arms and to the God of hosts is all that is left us!*

"They tell us, sir, that we are weak; unable to cope with so formidable an adversary. But when shall we be stronger? Will it be the next week, or the next year? Will it be when we are totally disarmed, and when a British guard shall be stationed in every house? Shall we gather strength by irresolution and inaction? Shall we acquire the means of effectual resistance by lying supinely on our backs and hugging the delusive phantom of hope, until our enemies shall have bound us hand and foot? Sir, we are not weak if we make a proper use of those means *which the God of nature* hath placed in our power. The millions of people, armed in the holy cause of liberty, and in such a country as that which we possess, are invincible by any force which our enemy can send against us. *Besides, sir, we shall not fight our battles alone. There is a just God who presides over the destinies of nations, and who will raise up friends to fight our battles for us.* The battle, sir, is not to the strong alone; it is to the vigilant, the active, the brave. ... What is it that gentlemen wish? What would they have? Is life so dear, or peace so sweet, as to be purchased at the price of chains and slavery? *Forbid it, Almighty God!* I know not what course others may take; but as for me, ***GIVE ME LIBERTY OR GIVE ME DEATH!***"

What gave birth to this patriot's "fightin' words" was his fear of God and his faith in God.

How did Mr. Henry refer to God? Re-read and underline: *"the majesty of heaven, the God of hosts, the God of nature, a just God, Almighty God!"* What an outstanding and *uncommon* combination! This influential Founding Father was not a deist: he was a Christian! He could no more submit to tyrannical government than he could to the devil. Patrick Henry had a spine.

Three famous speeches in American history tower above the rest, and *all three* are soaked in Scripture! The three are: Patrick Henry, *Give Me Liberty or Give Me Death*; Abraham Lincoln, *Gettysburg Address*; and Dr. Martin Luther King Jr., *I Have a Dream*.

Abraham Lincoln gave his *Gettysburg Address* (that children used to have to memorize) in November, 1863.

"Four score and seven years ago our fathers brought forth on this continent, **a new nation, conceived in Liberty, and dedicated to the proposition that all men are created equal.** *Now we are engaged in a great civil war, testing whether that nation, or any nation so conceived and so dedicated, can long endure. We are met on a great battle-field of that war. We have come to dedicate a portion of that field, as a final resting place for those who here gave their lives that that nation might live. It is altogether fitting and proper that we should do this. But, in a larger sense, we cannot dedicate—we cannot consecrate—we cannot hallow -- this ground. The brave men, living and dead, who struggled here, have consecrated it, far above our poor power to add or detract. The world will little note, nor long remember what we say here, but it can never forget what they did here. It is for us the living, rather, to be dedicated here to the unfinished work which they who fought here have thus far so nobly advanced. It is rather for us to be here dedicated to the great task remaining before us—that from these honored dead we take increased devotion to that cause for which they gave the last full measure of devotion—that we here highly resolve that these dead shall not have died in vain—* **that this nation, UNDER GOD, shall have a new birth of freedom—and that government of the people, by the people, for the people, shall not perish from the earth."**

Young people: **God and America are inseparable! You can't have America without God!**

You might ask, "What about "separation of church and state"?

You have to grasp this: Whatever *separation of church and state* means it cannot cancel out what *under God* means.

For the last 70 plus years, the Supreme Court has used the separation phrase to secularize America, to create a hostile environment against Christianity.

SEPARATION ... RE-THOUGHT

Who originated the phrase, *separation of church and state*?

It was Christian preachers who did not want the State to persecute them for their Christianity!

These preachers understood the Bible, which separated the three offices of prophet, priest, and king in the nation of Israel; that is, the king was never the priest and could not control the priest or the prophet. These preachers knew the history of both Catholic and Protestant persecution of other Christians, and in the words of Rev. Roger Williams in 1644, they wanted *"a hedge or wall of separation between the garden of the Church and the wilderness of the world."*[27]

Jefferson used the phrase when writing to Christians, who had supported him in his run for the Presidency, to assure them that the Federal Government would *in no way* interfere with the free exercise of their faith in God. His letter, dated 1802, reads as follows:

"Believing with you that religion is a matter which lies solely between man and his God, that he owes account to none other for his faith or his worship, that the legislative powers of government reach actions only, and not opinions, I contemplate with sovereign reverence that act of the whole American people which declared that their legislature would 'make no law respecting an establishment of religion, or prohibiting the free exercise thereof,' **thus building a wall of separation between Church and State.**"

---

[27] David Barton, *The Jefferson Lies*, WND Books, Washington, D.C., 2012,2016, p. 154.

Thomas Jefferson's original intent was that the wall kept the Federal Government out of the Church—it did not keep the Church silenced, suppressed and sidelined. His wall limited the powers of the Federal Government—not the powers of the Church.

To understand *separation of church and state* as mandating nationwide atheism is a gross perversion of the phrase.

Separation does *not* mean that each State cannot promote Christianity, or require the Bible as a textbook, or give time for prayer in our public schools. Anti-Christian rulings by the Supreme Court all stem from its disastrous ruling in 1947, in which Justice Hugo Black invoked Jefferson's metaphor but *reversed* what Jefferson had originally intended, *upending* the First Amendment! Jefferson *never* envisioned or desired a secular State imposing a gag order on Christianity. He *never* intended that his wall would bring down on America the revolting spectacle of atheistic indoctrination.[28]

"Tear down this wall!" President Ronald Reagan challenged the Soviet leader Gorbachev in 1987. The Berlin Wall was a symbol of government as god and the denial of freedom.

Today, it is time to tear down the Supreme Court's bogus wall of separation of church and state.

We do need Jefferson's wall—the wall that keeps the government in its proper place, *out* of the church. Why? *Preaching the Gospel is not a privilege, it is a right.* It is a God-given right. God alone gives rights. Though sinners will submissively accept authoritarian government in exchange for "free stuff"—we must not! *Preaching the Gospel of the Lord Jesus Christ is our God-given right, enshrined in our Constitution, that neither the federal government, nor any local, county or state government can legitimately suspend, revoke or curtail.*

39

---

[28] Get ALL the facts: read *The Jefferson Lies*, Lie #5. The 1947 Supreme Court decision was *Everson v. Board of Education*.

President Ronald Reagan said:

"Freedom is never more than one generation away from extinction. We didn't pass it to our children in the bloodstream. It must be fought for protected, and handed on for them to do the same."[29]

Wake up, young people of America! Never be satisfied with dumbed-down indoctrination that leaves you vulnerable to lying tyrants and slick-talking politicians!

THE REAL THOMAS JEFFERSON

Some assert that President Jefferson was a hypocritical slave-holding racist, a deist or worse. Learn to question the accepted "facts"—the "narrative" you are supposed to believe.

In 1776, Jefferson wrote the following anti-slavery grievance in his draft of the *Declaration of Independence* (a clause that he was unfortunately compelled to delete by some southern states):

"He [the King of England] has waged cruel war against human nature itself, violating its most sacred rights of life and liberty in the person of a distant people who never offended him, captivating & carrying them into slavery in another hemisphere, or to incur miserable death in their transportation thither ... he has prostituted his negative [his veto power] for suppressing every legislative attempt to prohibit or to restrain this execrable commerce."[30]

Jefferson knew that slavery was incompatible with the American Dream.

In 1781, still deeply distressed about slavery and being fully persuaded that God made all people to be free, Jefferson wrote:

---

[29] From Reagan's California Gubernatorial Speech, January 5, 1967
[30] Barton, *The Jefferson Lies*, p. 135; quoting Thomas Jefferson, *The Papers of Thomas Jefferson.* Vol. 1, 1760-1776

"The whole commerce between master and slave is a perpetual exercise of the most boisterous passions, the most unremitting despotism on the one part, and degrading submissions on the other ... And with what execration should the statesman be loaded, who permitting one half the citizens thus to trample on the rights of the other, transforms those into despots, and these into enemies, *destroys the morals of the one part*, and the amor patriae of the other ... [Amor patriae is love of country.] And CAN THE LIBERTIES OF A NATION BE THOUGHT SECURE WHEN WE HAVE REMOVED THEIR ONLY FIRM BASIS, A CONVICTION IN THE MINDS OF THE PEOPLE THAT THESE LIBERTIES ARE OF THE GIFT OF GOD? That they are not to be violated but with his wrath? Indeed I tremble for my country when I reflect that God is just: that his justice cannot sleep for ever: considering numbers, nature and natural means only, a revolution of the wheel of fortune, an exchange of situation, is among possible events: that it may become probable by *supernatural interference! The Almighty* has no attribute which can take sides with us in such a contest ... The spirit of the master is abating, that of the slave rising from the dust, his condition mollifying, the way I hope preparing, *under the auspices of heaven,* for a total emancipation, and that this is disposed, in the order of events, to be with the consent of the masters, rather than by their extirpation."[31]

Supernatural interference?! The Almighty?! The gift of God?! His wrath?! The auspices of heaven?!

Are these the sentiments of an irreligious, calloused man who wanted God shut out of public life and kept confined within the walls of the church? No.

41

---

[31] Ibid., p. 137; quoting Thomas Jefferson, *Notes on the State of Virginia*, 1781, Query 18

Truth is, Jefferson wanted emancipation. He knew that God was watching the nation. He knew that slavery was an act of treason against the hopes of the world. He wrote, *"We are not in a world ungoverned by the laws and the power of a Superior Agent."*[32] A heartless Deist? I don't think so.

YES: *A CHRISTIAN* NATION!

In 1892, by unanimous verdict, the Supreme Court issued a profound ruling. The case is *Church of the Holy Trinity v. United States*, and it overturned the deportation of a preacher (yes, some were trying to kick a preacher out of our country!). In 1880, Congress had passed a law prohibiting the importation of manual laborers, to prevent the lowering of wages. The Court ruled: *"No one would suppose that Congress had in its mind any purpose of staying the coming into this country of ministers of the gospel ... the intent of Congress was simply to stay the influx of this cheap unskilled labor."* Now, the Court could have stopped here, but it is hugely significant that it did not. The Court continued:

> *"But, beyond all these* [legal] *matters, no purpose of action against religion can be imputed to any legislation, state or national, because **this is a religious people**. This is historically true. **From the discovery of this continent to the present hour, there is a single voice making this affirmation.**"*

The Court then cited the following as proof of our nation's godly heritage: the commission to Columbus, the colonial grant to Raleigh, the First Charter of Virginia, the Mayflower Compact, the Fundamental Orders of Connecticut, the *Declaration of Independence*, all 44 state constitutions, and finally, the Constitution of the United States, and concluded:

42

---

[32] Ibid., p. 142.

"If we examine the constitutions of the various states, we find in them *a constant recognition of religious obligations*. Every Constitution of every one of the forty-four states contains language which recognizes *a profound reverence for religion*, and *an assumption that its influence in all human affairs is essential to the wellbeing of the community*. Even the Constitution of the United States contains in the First Amendment a declaration common to the constitutions of all the states, as follows: "Congress shall make no law respecting an establishment of religion, or prohibiting the free exercise thereof," and also provides in Article I, Section 7, a provision common to many constitutions, that the executive shall have ten days (Sundays excepted) within which to determine whether he will approve or veto is a universal language pervading them all, having one meaning a bill. *There is no dissonance in these declarations. There. They affirm and reaffirm that this is a religious nation. These are not individual sayings, declarations of private persons. They are organic utterances. They speak the voice of the entire people. ... we are a Christian people, and the morality of the country is deeply engrafted upon Christianity* ... If we pass beyond these matters to a view of American life, as expressed by its laws, its business, its customs, and its society, we find everywhere a clear recognition of the same truth ... These, and many other matters which might be noticed, add a volume of unofficial declarations to the mass of organic utterances that <u>THIS IS A CHRISTIAN NATION</u>."[33]

To say that America is a Christian nation is to say that Christianity is America's DNA: it forms our core identity; it directs our destiny, it creates our future.

To say that America is a Christian nation is to say that America was founded by believers in Jesus Christ for the express purpose of worshipping and serving God freely.

---

[33] The unanimous verdict was written by Justice David Brewer.

Young People, Re-Think!

To say that America is a Christian nation is to say that America was built on a Judeo-Christian foundation.

Let the uninformed understand that Christianity cannot be separated from its Jewish roots or its Jewish Savior, and that real Christianity is never anti-Semitic.

Let everyone understand that America was not, is not, and never will be, an atheistic nation!

AMERICA IS NOW AND ALWAYS WILL BE ONE NATION *UNDER GOD!*

BEWARE BLIND GUIDES!

Reason is a God-given tool, but reason is not god. Reason must have the right premises, or it will lead you hopelessly astray.

The greatest premise is that there is a God, and you are not Him! College can be a good thing (provided you don't drown in debt), but college is not church. Let me put it together in one sentence: *Reason is not god and college is not church.*

You must realize that in *Jesus* are hid *all* the treasures of wisdom and knowledge.

You must identify and spurn blind guides. That's what Jesus wants you to do. He warned His disciples, referring to the Pharisees, saying, *"Let them alone; they be blind leaders of the blind. And if the blind lead the blind, both shall fall into the ditch."* Later, Jesus directly rebuked the Pharisees: *"Ye BLIND GUIDES, which strain at a gnat, and swallow a camel."*[34]

Why were the Pharisees blind guides? Mostly because they put all their attention on the outside, but neglected the heart. God looks at our heart.

44

---

[34] Matthew 16:14; 23:24

Blind guides will tell you about "esoteric" secrets of the "New Age" reserved for "advanced souls" which are, in fact, nothing but rehashed lies from 18th century "Enlightenment", 19th century "New Thought" and 1st century Gnosticism, mixed with Hinduism and Zen Buddhism.

Beware the flattery of blind guides! It is very appealing to your ego to think of yourself as an "advanced soul" with "higher consciousness." Please. Reality check! You have *not* lived before; you are not an evolved soul. Sorry to burst your bubble.

Let me make it plain so you can't claim, "I misunderstood."

Reincarnation is a lie, a hoax and a doctrine of devils.

Evolution is a lie, perpetrated by atheistic scientists.

Science, we 100% believe in; but atheistic science, with its denial of God and its millions (or billions!) of years for us to evolve from nothing by time and chance, we firmly reject.

There are two dangers; the first is despiritualizing life; the second is embracing spirituality but shunning Jesus.

First. You are not just mind and body. God is a Spirit; He has a mind. You are a spiritual being, made in God's image. It is with our spirit that we contact God and receive His love and His life. You are spirit, soul and body.

Second. There is a lie persuading many: "I'm spiritual but not religious." I say: Spirituality without obedience to the God of the Bible is a farce. Yes, be spiritual: but the spirit world is filled with deceivers and demons, eager to prey on the naïve.

The paranormal is a sinkhole; the occult is quicksand. Any "religion" that demotes Jesus to a mere man is a devilish cult. Beware! Jesus warned that *deception* would be a sign of the end. How do you avoid deception?

(1)   You hold to Jesus.
(2)   You hold to the Bible.
(3)   You stay in church.
(4)   You stay humble.

Jesus Christ is fully God, and He became Man. He had a literal flesh and blood body; He literally died for our sin and then literally rose from the dead to die no more.

If you get any supposed "revelation" from an "avatar" or "guru" or in a dream, submit it to your Pastor; let him judge it. Stay connected to other believers in the local church; do not become a loner. Choose friends who are in church, who want the things of God, not the counterfeits of this world. Above all, have the *uncommon sense* to build your life on the Bible!

If you know Jesus, you must change the culture, using every social platform to say what is worthwhile, not what is worthless. Sinners must become like you: you must not become like them. You must influence them and lead them to Jesus. They may be "cool" with totalitarian rule; you must never be. They may buy every flagrant lie; you must not. You must be a history-maker, a difference-maker!

If you don't know Jesus, humble yourself today while Jesus is tenderly calling: "Come unto Me!" and knocking at the door of your heart. You can encounter Jesus today! When you take Jesus as your Lord and come under His authority, He will lift you up—out of sin and into your God-given destiny. *Take Jesus now!* You hear a lot about climate change, but climate change is not mankind's biggest threat: *sin* is. Jesus alone has the cure for sin and sin's pollution: His own precious blood. He, the risen Lord Jesus Christ, will create a new heaven and a new earth in which sin and death are no more. If you have Jesus, you have a future. And, if you partner with Jesus:

America will be saved!

4

TRUTH & FREEDOM

Jesus said, "Thy Word is Truth."[35]

**"They received not *the love of the Truth*,
that they might be saved. For this cause
God shall send them *strong delusion*,
that they should believe a lie:
that they all might be damned
who believed not the Truth,
but had pleasure in unrighteousness."**[36]

Were you to visit our nation's colleges and universities, you would think that Truth has either disappeared or dropped dead, and you might even cry out in despair, along with the prophet of old, *"Truth is fallen in the street!"*[37]

Freedom and Truth are inseparable. You can't be free without Truth. Freedom cannot survive where Truth is absent; it cannot thrive where Truth is suppressed. What is Truth?

---

[35] John 17:17
[36] 2 Thessalonians 2:10-12
[37] Isaiah 59:14

Truth is not a synthesis of your opinion and my opinion. Truth is not something we get to vote on or invent. You don't get to make up your own truth or decide what is true for you. Truth is the same for everybody. Truth is absolute not obsolete. Truth is not subjective. Truth is universal, authoritative and objective. Truth is eternal and immutable. Truth is timeless and transcendent. Truth is trans-cultural and trans-generational. Truth is always true and it covers the totality of our lives: it is the first word and the final word in every area of life. Truth does not evolve: it is either forever true or it is never true. Truth is not a moveable object. Truth is not fluid. Truth does not become untrue just because you don't like it or don't agree with it, any more than the sun stops shining because you stick your head in a bucket. Truth is not a dead philosophy about which you argue. Truth is a living Person before whom you bow. *Jesus is the Truth.*

His Word is forever settled.

- *"God is dead"* is a lie.
- *"Everything is relative"* is a lie.
- *"Everything evolves"* is a lie.
- *"We can't know anything for certain"* is a lie.
- *"There is no such thing as absolute truth"* is a lie.
- *"This life is all there is"* is a lie.

Atheism is an angry assault on Truth.

Why does this matter to the United States of America?

Our *Declaration of Independence* unequivocally proclaimed self-evident truths: *"endowed by their Creator."*

But if the Creator is dead, then Truth is dead. If Truth is dead, then self-evident truths are also dead. If self-evident truths are replaced by lying atheistic theories, then America is dead. If Truth is dead, then freedom is dead. It comes down to this:

If God is dead, then America is dead.

But God is not dead. God is alive. And Truth is alive. Therefore, *America can live.*

God's Truth is the stabilizing force of life. God's Word is Truth. To remove God's Word is to destabilize society. To eliminate God's Truth is to be left with demonic wisdom and demonic solutions that solve nothing. Unprincipled journalists, politicians, educators and business folk prefer lies to Truth and anarchy to stability, so that they can grab power. Can you see why Truth is priceless? Truth is the foundation of great nations.

Self-evident truths, upon which America was built, spring out of God's revealed Truth. Free government comes out of hearts set free by Truth. Over the last several decades, we have tried, unsuccessfully, to "export democracy," despite our military might. *Uncommon sense* sees why. *To try to plant democracy in nations lacking a Christian base is the equivalent of trying to plant flowers on concrete.*

The Bible is the Ultimate Freedom Book. The Bible is the Source and Standard of Truth. All opinions must be measured against this divine, infallible standard. Any system of reasoning, philosophy or religion that ignores, contradicts or defies Scripture Truth has as much worth and durability as a child's sandcastle by the ocean. The Bible is absolute, forever-settled Truth. The Bible is right about everything, because it is *God's* holy Word. The Psalmist was correct when he prayed, *"I esteem all Thy precepts concerning all things to be right; and I hate every false way."*[38]

Jesus said, *"I AM the Truth."*[39] His full statement is even more categorical: *"I AM the Way, the Truth, and the Life: no man cometh unto the Father, but by Me."* Had Jesus said, "I am *a* way—just one of many—there are really many ways to God," He would have been politically correct, but a liar.

49

---

[38] Psalm 119:128
[39] John 14:6

You may not like what Jesus says or understand it, but that does not change Him or negate His words. Was Jesus being a bit too "full of Himself"? Or, was He telling the whole truth and nothing but the truth? *Why* did He say that He was the *only* Way? I answer: Only Jesus shed His own sinless blood. Without sinless blood shed on our behalf, our sins cannot be expunged and we have no access to God. Since all of us have sinned, our blood is defiled. There is only ONE who did not sin: JESUS. No other human being has sinless blood to offer: we are all sinners in need of a Savior and His cleansing blood. Atheistic philosophy will not save us from the bondage and the consequences of our sin. No psychological treatment can remove the pain, the shame and the slavery of our sin. We can stubbornly deny our sin ... but that is self-delusion and self-damnation.

I come face-to-face with Jesus' astounding claim that He is THE Way. Jesus is either a liar, a lunatic, a legend—or He is Lord. I assert: **Jesus is Lord.** I testify: **Jesus is *my* Lord.** Jesus is either a dead imposter—or He is the risen Son of God. I proclaim: ***He lives and He lives in me!***

Jesus said, *"If ye continue in My Word, then are ye My disciples indeed; and ye shall know the Truth, and the Truth shall make you free."*[40]

Sin is a tyrant. Those who are enslaved by this tyrant willingly accept tyrannical government. Only those who know the Truth, who are liberated from the tyranny of sin, are ready to throw off tyrannical government—because only they know God as their loving Father. He meets their deepest needs! In order to know the Truth, you must continue in Jesus' Word. If you ignore Jesus and scoff at His Word, you deprive yourself of Truth, freedom, and a relationship with God the Father. You may know certain truths, but you will be a stranger to Truth, and you will be susceptible to deception.

50

---

[40] John 8:31-32

Atheistic socialism is today's #1 deception.

Moments before He was crucified, Jesus told the Roman governor, *"For this cause came I into the world, that I should bear witness unto the Truth. Everyone that is of the Truth heareth My voice."* Pilate retorted, *"What is Truth?"*[41]As if to say, with his philosophical pomposity, "No one can ever know Truth." Is that so?! Truth ever eludes those impressed with their own intellect.

You must choose between Pilate's relativism and Jesus' reality. It is the choice between death and life, between bondage and freedom, between ignorance and illumination. Everyone who is a sincere lover of Truth will—sooner or later—gladly listen to Jesus, take His words as absolute Truth and put them into practice.

The result of knowing Truth is freedom: first, freedom from the guilt, misery and grip of sin, and second, freedom from the imposed fiats of a pompous atheistic elite who think they know better than you, who delight in ordering you around and penalizing you when you dare disagree.

Knowing Truth has two invaluable benefits: the first is spiritual, the second, political.

To my secular-minded fellow-citizens: If you want the second but not the first, you can't have the second, because the second is built on the first. If you grasp that, and want the first, first, you are beginning to demonstrate that exceptional quality: *uncommon sense.*

If you want freedom from oppressive government, but want nothing to do with the moral government of God, you are chasing smoke.

Only those who voluntarily come under the righteous moral government of Almighty God are fit to be free politically.

51

---

[41] John 18:37,38

Only those who embrace the freedom from sin that Jesus graciously provides, are ready to embrace the responsibility of free government.

Jesus called the devil a liar and a murderer. It is the devil who wants to deceive and destroy individuals and divide nations, and lies are his weapon of choice. Understand: God did not make the devil. God made a perfect, sinless angelic being full of wisdom. This created being became the devil by his own choice because he did not glorify God for the wisdom he possessed. The devil corrupted his God-given wisdom in order to exalt himself above God.

There is God's everlasting Truth: it is life-giving and freedom-forming; and there are the devil's slick lies: sophisticated, but death-dealing and freedom-undoing.

Today we must **choose** one or the other.

My fellow Americans: We must choose Truth and holiness! *If we do not humble ourselves under God and embrace His absolute Truth and His fixed principles of right and wrong, we will be forced to drink the bitter cup of atheistic socialism year after year until all our prosperity is evaporated and all our liberties are faded memories.* If we do not regain our love of the Truth, our fear of God and our moral sanity, terrible sentence will be passed on America as it was passed on Babylon before that once glorious empire sank into oblivion: *"Thou art weighed in the balances, and art found wanting."*[42]

As for me, I want a better future than atheists or socialists or self-appointed experts can provide. I do not believe that America is destined to share the sad fate of Babylon. I believe:

America will be saved!

---

[42] Daniel 5:27

5

WORLDVIEW & ETHICS

**The wicked shall be turned into hell,
and all the nations that forget God.**[43]

Your ethics flow out of your worldview.

Your worldview is your way of looking at life.

Your worldview consists of your answers to big and basic questions: How did life begin? How did the universe come into existence? How did I get here? Who am I? Why am I here? What is my destiny? What is my purpose? Why is there death? What happens after I die? Is there a God? What is sin? How do I get rid of guilt? Is there a Judgment Day? What is my moral standard? What is the nature of God? Is He present and involved, or disinterested and detached?

Your worldview not only forms your ethics, it shapes your ideology.

Ideologies produce governments.

---

[43] Psalm 9:17

Bad ideologies produce tyrannical governments with unlimited power that result in oppression, poverty and the slaughter of the innocent.

Good ideologies produce governments with limited powers that promote opportunity, prosperity, freedom under law and equal justice for all.

A worldview is comprehensive; it ought to be coherent.

The Christian worldview:

- produces triumphant hope in the face of death
- produces moral character in the face of temptation
- produces dignity, worth and value for every person.

The atheistic worldview cannot produce these three things, and therefore, is glaringly deficient. Atheism offers no resurrection, no grace, and no rational basis to value all people.

Does it matter what I believe?

It absolutely does.

Hitler drew from the poisoned wells of Marx and Nietzsche.

Americans ought to draw from the well that our Founding Fathers drew from: *The Bible.*

"IN THE BEGINNING ..."

"In the beginning, God created the heaven and the earth."[44]

This is the first sentence of the Bible. This is NOT "divine theory." The Bible is not archaic religious theory: it is pertinent Truth. Man did not make our universe. *God* did.

---

[44] Genesis 1:1

God was never man. God was never not-God. God was God, is God, and always will be God. God everlastingly is, whether He created anything or not. God chose to create.

"And God said, Let us make man in our image."[45] God the Father is speaking with God the Son and God the Holy Spirit. There is one God; "God in three Persons, blessed Trinity."

Man was made by God in the image of God. Man speaks because God speaks. Man has a moral nature because God is a moral Being. *"So God created man in His own image, in the image of God created He him; male and female created He them."*[46] Men and women are equal in the sight of God.

The forever fact that God made us in His image is what gives us our inestimable value.

If, as atheism teaches, we are nothing but dust made by time and chance, then we are all expendable and disposable. *But that is a lie.* As for me, I prefer the Truth. I love the Truth! Is man merely mind and molecules? No. Scripture says: *"And I pray God your whole spirit and soul and body be preserved blameless unto the coming of our Lord Jesus Christ."*[47]So then, man is far more than mind and molecules. Man is a spirit being, because God is a Spirit. God is not "cosmic Mind." God has a mind, but He is a Spirit. I contact God with my spirit. I believe with my spirit. I think with my mind. My body is the house in which I live. *I believe therefore I am!* I am not an evolved anything. I have value that no man can diminish.

God did not create you to be minimized, maligned, mistreated, manipulated or muted. He created you to rule! He did not create you to be bullied, to be terrorized or to live in fear. He created you to reign in this life and in the next!

---

[45] Genesis 1:26
[46] Genesis 1:27
[47] 1 Thessalonians 5:23

Calm down: you do not rule over people. No one is your slave.

You are destined to reign, first of all, over *sin*. *How* will you do that? By the almighty grace of God.

When you are ruling over sin by grace, you become able to fulfill your destiny *under God*. You become part of the restraining power—the true Church—that refuses to let an antichrist globalist government take power. The devil wants you to sin so that you thereby forfeit your dominion over him and his wicked schemes. But now you are wise to his tactics!

Now, just as the Lord Jesus Christ is forever opposed to the devil, so the ideology of atheism/socialism is incompatible with the ideology of Christianity—*they cannot co-exist*. One or the other must become dominant.

Three observations about the atheistic worldview and its lying presuppositions: *"There is no god. Man is God."*

First, this worldview produces an ethical system that is subject only to the whim of the elite who hold it. Second, this system allows for any behavior, no matter how abhorrent, appalling or abominable. Third, these elite are arrogantly intolerant of anyone who opposes them, and will, without hesitation or regret, use all the powers of the state either to coerce compliance, silence dissent or eliminate any stubborn opposition.

Therefore, the atheistic worldview brings about national nightmare: government *on* the people, *over* the people, *against* the people: the *exact opposite* of the American Dream.

If there is no God, then there is no such thing as sin: literally anything can be justified.

But when sin and God's moral law disappear, then freedom is hijacked by demons who turn it into a license to perpetrate the worst wickedness.

In atheistic culture, sin is gone (unless you say that chocolate is 'sinfully delicious'). Language becomes a tool in the hands of the elite, who attack dissenters by using the very terminology native in the opposing Christian worldview.

For example, a border wall is said to be immoral.

Standing against abortion is declared to be shameful.

The words *immoral* and *shameful* have no rational place in the atheistic worldview, yet they are used as attack words by the atheistic elite to promote their own dark, sinful agenda.

WHAT IS SIN?

Sin is war against God.

The goal of this war is the elimination of God and the annihilation of the moral authority of God.

Sin is self-rule. Sin is self as god. Sin is rebellion against the moral law of God. Sin is rejection of the moral authority of God. Sin is spitting in God's holy face. Sin is dishonoring, despising and defying the one, true living God.

Sin, *singular*, gives birth to sins, *plural*. Sins are specific acts of disobedience against God and His moral law, or any neglect of His moral commands.

Sin is a liar: it promises happiness, but delivers bondage. Sin is inherently immoral, always causes shame and always brings death. Sin imprisons the soul in an invisible cage. Every sinner is bound by chains of his own making, chains he cannot break—chains only Jesus can break!

Thank God, America is not an *anti-God* nation, a nation deceived by sin and bound in the chains of sin. America is a free nation, because millions of Americans have been set free from sin by Jesus Christ.

In the Christian worldview, there is a God. God is our Creator, our Law-Giver and our Judge. In the Christian worldview, the will of God flows from the wisdom of God. The moral law of God expresses the holy moral nature of God. God is love and God is holy. God will never, for even a moment, become 'non-love' or deviate from love and holiness. God's moral law is the righteous reflection of His heart of love and of His holy character. God forbids murder (which is what abortion is) because He is a life-giver. He forbids stealing because He is a giver. He forbids adultery because He is faithful. He forbids bearing false witness because He cannot lie. He forbids covetousness because He is more than enough. The moral laws of God maximize our freedom and happiness.

God's morality is not fluid. It does not evolve. It is immutable. Therefore, His moral laws are absolute. His moral laws are not arbitrary; rather, they harmonize perfectly with His love and holiness. Every action is either moral or immoral, ethical or unethical, when judged in the light of the law of love. The royal law of love is used as the determiner of what is righteous or wicked. That's *uncommon sense*.

In his 1789 *First Inaugural Address*, President George Washington spoke what today would be considered bigoted:

"The propitious smiles of Heaven can never be expected on a nation that disregards the eternal rules of order and right, which Heaven itself has ordained."

Eternal rules are rules that do not change. To eject God and His eternal rules is to adopt the immorality of demons.

President Washington had the happy vision of God smiling on America, but he had enough *uncommon sense* to know that God's smile would turn into tears if the nation disdained God's moral authority and ran recklessly after sin.

Morality is either based on reality and truth—or on lies, misinformation and opinions.

Policy is based on morality.

Legislation enforces someone's morality.

We must have right laws, but in order to have right laws, we must have right hearts. Laws prohibit certain behaviors, but laws cannot change hearts. Only love can change the heart.

Only the love of God entering and overwhelming the human heart can bring about lasting behavioral change.

Atheism has no power to change a selfish heart into a loving heart—only Christianity does.

No man-made religion has the power to cause a greedy, selfish, hate-bound sinner to love his enemies. Man does not have the power to change his own heart. He cannot obey Jesus' Sermon on the Mount in his own strength. He must have the almighty grace of God.

AMAZING, ALMIGHTY GRACE

Only Jesus gives us grace, which is God's undeserved favor *and* unlimited ability.

Grace is not God's permission to sin nor His pass when we sin; grace is His power working in us so we stop sinning. Grace is the power of the Holy Spirit, His ability and aid that empowers us to obey God's moral law of love and do what is right in God's sight.

Grace produces true beauty of soul. Grace makes the impossible possible.

Perhaps you are surprised to read that grace is "almighty." One of our problems is that we have done in the church what the world has done in our schools: there has been a "dumbing down" of vital information. To see grace *only* as favor, unmerited favor, is to run off with a half-definition.

A god of cheap grace who gives a gospel without blood to sinners without repentance so they can live without moral restraints and face eternity without judgment—is a false god! We must reject a pseudo-gospel that accommodates our flesh and excuses our disobedience.

The true Gospel is not bloodless, powerless, lifeless philosophy. The true Gospel is not man-made psychological theory. The true Gospel did not come out of man's head. *The true Gospel came out of God's heart!* A heart of passionate love for us! The true Gospel gives us true grace, so we may be conformed to the moral image of the Lord Jesus Christ.

Without grace, all we can do is sin. Without grace, we can like those who like us, but we cannot love our sworn enemies. Muslims, for example, may love other Muslims, provided they are of the same sect, but there is nothing in Islamic Jihad to empower Muslims to love Jews, Hindus or Christians. Neither Islam nor atheism has grace. The more our culture becomes atheistic, the more graceless and the uglier we become.

God wept over the nation of Israel before they were swept away into Babylonian captivity: *"For My people have committed two evils; they have forsaken Me the Fountain of Living Waters, and hewed them out cisterns, broken cisterns, that can hold no water."*[48] What a horrible trade!

Now you can understand why there are so many murders and atrocities in our nation: we have traded the love of God and the grace of God for atheism. When we undo this trade by repenting of our sin and coming under the Lordship of Jesus:

America will be saved!

---

[48] Jeremiah 2:13

6

WHY ATHEISM WON'T WORK

The fool has said in his heart, "There is no God."[49]

"Be still, and know that I am God."[50]

"Before Me there was no god formed, neither shall there be after Me. I, even I, am the LORD; and beside Me there is no Savior."[51]

It is folly to say there is no God, lunacy to think there is no eternity, and insanity to live as if there is no Judgment Day.

Atheism is lunacy on steroids.

Atheism provides no basis to treat other human beings with dignity and respect and tenderness. Dogs and cats may actually be esteemed more highly than babies or old folk or the disabled. This exposes the rotten core of atheism.

Self is the god of atheism. "God self" will conjure up a morality suited to the basest desires and can never produce the sterling moral character necessary for free government.

---

[49] Psalm 14:1
[50] Psalm 46:10
[51] Isaiah 43:10-11

In his 1796 *Farewell Address*, President George Washington wrote the following about *morality* and *religion*; *religion* being a reference to *Christianity*. It is a long quote but foundational; therefore, please persevere:

"Of all the dispositions and habits which lead to political prosperity, *religion and morality* are indispensable supports. In vain would that man claim the tribute of patriotism who should labor to subvert *these great pillars of human happiness*—these firmest props of the duties of men and citizens. The mere politician, equally with the pious man, ought to respect and to cherish them. A volume could not trace all their connections with private and public felicity. Let it simply be asked: Where is the security for property, for reputation, for life, if the sense of religious obligation desert the oaths which are the instruments of investigation in courts of justice? *And let us with caution indulge the supposition that morality can be maintained without religion.* Whatever may be conceded to the influence of refined education on minds of peculiar structure, *reason and experience both forbid us to expect that national morality can prevail in exclusion of religious principle.*"

Washington, with *uncommon wisdom*, called Christianity and morality the pillars of happiness.

To the reprobate mind, Christianity and morality are the very things that must be eliminated in order to pursue happiness.

President Washington did not have a reprobate mind. He understood that a people must be moral in order to be free. Without Christianity and morality, people exchange their duty for debauchery. Morality flows out of Christianity. Morality severed from Christianity is like cut flowers: it seems beautiful for a time, but it will soon wither, being severed from its life-source. Only Jesus can change the stone-cold heart and cause the new heart to love purity.

A loving moral code flows out of a heart filled with the love of God. Together, morality and Christianity produce liberty and prosperity. Therefore, if we reject morality and Christianity, we undermine the foundation of freedom.

A contemporary of George Washington, Edmund Burke, five years before Washington penned his *Farewell Address*, wrote the following:

> *"Men are qualified for civil liberty in exact proportion to their disposition to put moral chains upon their own appetites;* in proportion as their love of justice is above their rapacity—in proportion as their soundness and sobriety of understanding is above their vanity and presumption; in proportion as they are more disposed to listen to the counsels of the wise and good, in preference to the flattery of knaves. Society cannot exist unless a controlling power upon will and appetite be placed somewhere, and the less of it there is within, the more there must be without. *It is ordained in the eternal constitution of things, that men of intemperate minds cannot be free. Their passions forge their fetters."*[52]

If Burke was right, then men and women who have *no* disposition to put moral chains on their appetites are *dis*qualified from enjoying civil liberty. Why? Their rapacity annihilates their love of justice. Rapacity is the love of money.

If Burke was right, then men and women who have neither the time nor the desire to read the Holy Bible are *dis*qualified from enjoying "the land of the free." Why? Their understanding and foresight will be darkened by dishonesty, disinformation and deliberate dissimulation.

---

[52] Edmund Burke (1729-1797), *A Letter to a Member of the National Assembly*, 1791.

If Burke was right, then our generation—afflicted as it is with intemperate minds—cannot remain free. An intemperate mind is ungovernable and unrestrained: it despises moral boundaries. And while it may boast of its freedom, its freedom is a futile chasing after the wind, because *"It is ordained in the eternal constitution of things, that men of intemperate minds cannot be free."*

Who made "the eternal constitution of things"? There is only One who could have—One who is outside of time and space—the living God, the Eternal One! It is *His* eternal law that whoever sins, is the slave of sin. Try as you might, you cannot repeal or amend *that* law.

If Burke was right, then I as an individual have a choice: I can either have a controlling power *within,* or a controlling power *without.* The controlling power *within* can be the Holy Spirit, the love of God and the empowering grace of the Lord Jesus Christ. The controlling power *without* is the ruthless State.

Shudder, ponder, then decide for yourself.

America's second President, John Adams, proclaimed,

"We have no government armed with power capable of contending with human passions unbridled by morality and religion. *Our Constitution was made only for a moral and religious people.* It is wholly inadequate to the government of any other."[53]

Both Adams and Washington knew that America's *future* depended on the *morality* of American citizens.

---

[53] John Adams, *The Works of John Adams,* Second President of the United States Charles Frances Adams, editor (Boston: Little, Brown & Co., 1854), Vol. IX, p. 229, to the Officers of the First Brigade of the Third Division of the Militia of Massachusetts, October 11, 1798.

Both Adams and Washington knew that a revival of morality was impossible without a revival of religion. They knew that America had been birthed out of Great Awakening, a massive turning of the American people's hearts to God.

Only a *Great Awakening* will move us to give up the delusion that we are god, for the reality that it is best to be *under God*.

Only a *Great Awakening* will impel us to exchange our intemperate mind that rationalizes and relishes sin for the pure, holy, mind of Christ.

Only a *Great Awakening* will empower us to put chains on our moral appetites so that we need not ever wear any other chains.

Only a *Great Awakening* will remove from our hearts the love of money and instill in us a love for God, a love for all people, and a love of truth and justice.

Without a *Great Awakening*, "We the People" will keep on foolishly forging our own fetters. Without a *Great Awakening*, "We the People" will keep on drinking the cool aid of Marxism until we are imprisoned or eliminated for being "deplorable" or "undesirable."

But: a *Great Awakening* we will surely have, because:

America will be saved!

The ethical system that was the foundation of America consisted first of a vertical or God-ward dimension, and then of a horizontal dimension.

Ethics is more than how we humans relate to one another.

Ethics must include the fear of God.

Any ethical system that has no mention of our duties toward God our Creator and Judge is embarrassingly incomplete, and worse, strips away the security for property and life.

If *"We, the People"* have no fear of God, then no one is safe.

To adopt an ethical system devoid of a God-ward dimension is self-annihilation. Why? First, it leaves us under the grip of sin, in a state of selfishness, and therefore unable to do what is right toward others. Until our heart is won by the love of God, selfishness reigns. But when we receive the love of God, in comes the grace of God, the power of the Holy Spirit, which is power to love all people. Second, history teaches us that the atheistic ethical system that begins with the lying premise, *"There is no God. I am god"*—is a recipe for dictatorship. When self becomes god, then the State becomes god, and when that happens ... run for your life!

America is a great house supported by two solid pillars: Christianity and morality.

A free government cannot be upheld by the hollow posts of immorality and atheism.

A free government rests on the morality of its citizens; morality, in turn, springs from faith in the living God. This is all *uncommon sense*.

We need to grasp why atheism is pernicious.

Atheism is *inherently deceitful*. It is based on arrogant rejection of self-evident truth.

Atheism is *inherently intolerant*; it does not cherish free thought or free speech. Its preferred weapon is political correctness. Atheism seethes with diabolical hostility and deranged hatred against Christians and the Bible.

Atheism is *inherently immoral*. It has no conscience and no compunction about lying or killing in order to achieve its ends.

Atheism is *inherently degrading*. Atheists blaspheme and use profanity without hesitation. They have no fear of God.

Atheism is *inherently ruthless*. Two stark exhibits prove the ruthlessness of atheism. Exhibit A is Stalin, the atheistic Soviet dictator who murdered multiplied millions of his own countrymen. Exhibit B is abortion in America, where we have brutally murdered more than 60 million children.

Atheism is *inherently illegitimate*. Despising and refusing to come under God's legitimate authority, atheists have no authoritative basis for their opinions, morality or laws. Their only foundation is themselves.

Atheism always produces tyranny, and tyranny always produces poverty. Atheistic socialism cannot create wealth because it disincentivizes creativity and hard work; it creates instead, a crippling dependence on the State and a nauseating attitude of entitlement.

As a 'ship of state' atheistic socialism is as seaworthy as a tiny paper boat. Atheism would make Americans slaves of the state. To achieve this goal, atheists work to eliminate Christianity from public life and to revise the history of our nation, so shaming us with our nation's past sins that we jettison our God-given heritage and our God-given identity and destiny. Atheism always produces animosity and division; it cannot produce true love, since it is, in its core, a virulent hatred of God, who is love. Atheism produces a counterfeit of love: lust, and a counterfeit of liberty: licentiousness.

Today we see unfolding before our eyes the fulfillment of a dramatic prophecy by the prophet Isaiah, given 700 years before Christ—

"Woe unto them that call evil good, and good evil; that put darkness for light, and light for darkness; that put bitter for sweet, and sweet for bitter!"[54]

---

[54] Isaiah 5:20

What a tragedy it is when sin is called good and when wickedness is called sweet! What a disaster when holiness, which is good and sweet—is called evil and bitter! What a despicable lie when Christians, who love all people, are labelled 'hatemongers' or 'homophobes' because they do not meekly surrender to atheistic-immorality!

Today's atheistic elite would have us exchange the wisdom of God for the wisdom of demons. They would have us exchange trust in God for trust in government. They would have us exchange *uncommon sense* for their *nonsense.*

Atheism is not a sign of brilliance. Atheism is a sign of diseased wisdom. Atheism is irrational. It is supremely irrational to reject the God who cannot lie, and to trust the devil who does nothing but lie!

I reiterate: To remove God from His rightful place is to create a vacuum—and someone or something will fill that void: either an arrogant dictator like Hitler or Stalin—or the government with its various octopus branches that will surveil and mercilessly control every facet of your life.

If we throw God out of our lives, our ethics lose authority. If we remove God, we also remove His moral absolutes, and we are left with non-authoritative, conflicting opinions—held with arrogance and militant ferocity, but opinions nonetheless. Our ethics also lose stability because now they are based only on the whim of the elite— on whatever gratifies the elite. Furthermore, if we deliberately delete God from our lives, we become ruthless, brutal and cold-blooded. This must necessarily be the case. Why? If God is love, and He certainly is, then to delete God is to delete love. It is to separate ourselves from love, from Him who loves us, from the one true love that makes life worth living.

Moreover, to delete God is to delete hope, because God is a God of hope. Everyone needs hope for their future.

Secularists have no rational basis for hope: when they cut God out, they cut hope out and bring despair into their soul.

Jesus gives us living hope because He beat death! Since He did that, then He can create for us a future worth pursuing.

To delete God, is to delete all God gives. Pause and ponder. If deleting God sounds like the height of insanity to you, your *uncommon sense* is working!

When people lose their faith in God, their morality crumbles and they surrender their freedom to an ever more controlling state. The State, in the hands of the elite, becomes a weapon against anyone who dares to disagree. It is only when people stay *under God* that they are fit for freedom and use their freedom for good. When men and women want to play God, they become devils.

If you want a grim but realistic picture of our future under atheistic socialism, envision a spiked boot stomping on a human face: devil-driven humans arbitrarily deciding who is worthy to live and who is not. George Orwell had the keen foresight to write this in his book, *1984* (published in 1949). Orwell had the keen foresight to see where Communism was headed, but lacked the vital insight necessary to overcome atheistic tyranny—insight found only in Scripture.

Only believers authorized by the Lord Jesus Christ have authority over demons that try to subjugate people and nations.

Only believers who live right by grace can wield the scepter of righteousness and bring changes to their nation that God desires.

I want to close this chapter by referring to our First President and the first Inaugural Address. Prepare to be astonished. What you are about to read are not the words of a deist, and they are certainly not "politically correct."

"It would be peculiarly improper to omit in this first official Act, my fervent supplications to that *Almighty Being who rules over the Universe, who presides in the Councils of Nations, and whose providential aids can supply every human defect,* that His benediction may consecrate to the liberties and happiness of the People of the United States, a Government instituted by themselves for these essential purposes ... In tendering this homage to *the Great Author* of every public and private good I assure myself that it expresses your sentiments not less than my own ... No People can be bound to acknowledge and adore *the invisible Hand,* which conducts the Affairs of men, more than the People of the United States. Every step, by which they have advanced to the character of an independent nation, seems to have been distinguished *by some token of providential agency.*"

These are not the words of a "right win radical." They are the words of President George Washington, and they are a scathing rebuttal to the nonsense of atheism, to the pernicious idea that America is the land of atheism. It is God's invisible hand that has given America its leadership role in the world.

Only if we stay *under God* will we not squander our unique opportunity to lead the world.

We need to rethink what is going on in America while we still can speak up. Have you ever wondered what 'good' people were doing in Germany before Hitler grabbed power? When 'good' people do nothing, are they really good? We have one last window of opportunity to defy the atheistic elite, to combine *uncommon sense* with *uncommon dedication* to God, and to pray and work for a *Great Awakening* to God. *Time is running out!* Therefore, we must seize this now moment, because then and only then:

America will be saved!

7

PRO-LIFE

**Who will rise up for Me against the evildoers?
Or who will stand up for Me
against the workers of iniquity?**[55]

"You shall not murder."[56]

If you are reading this, one thing is undeniable: you were not aborted.

Morality has immense consequences.

Atheism produces a culture of death. Some assert: abortion is health care, social progress and every woman's right. Shameless lies!

Abortion is murder. Abortion is an unspeakably vile, barbaric atrocity, the despicable annihilation of the innocent. Abortion strips the unborn of all their God-given rights.

Abortion is as indefensible as slavery. **Abortion is just as wrong as slavery and racism, and is wrong for the same reasons.**

71

---

55 Psalm 94:16
56 The 6th Commandment, Exodus 20:13

Compare abortion with slavery and racism, using your *uncommon sense,* and you will see some embarrassingly shameful, uncomfortably painful parallels.

Imagine protestors and politicians with signs: "Keep slavery safe and legal!" Could you imagine that?

Now think ...

The slave trader and the slave owner *dehumanized* the slave. Today's atheistic elite want us to dehumanize the baby: to them it is not an unborn baby, it is "fetal tissue." The slave was not a person but property. The body of the slave did not matter; the will of the slave was not a consideration; any searing emotional pain the slave felt by being forcibly separated from his or her family was irrelevant. To the atheistic elite, the body of the baby does not matter; the will of the baby is not a consideration; any pain felt by the baby is irrelevant.

When pro-abortionists scream for their right to abort innocent babies, how is it any different than racist southern slavers of yesteryear demanding their white privilege to enslave blacks?

If you cannot justify making any man or woman a slave, how can you justify aborting a defenseless baby?

Slavery and racism did horrible damage to the helpless victims. But abortion, like slavery and racism, does permanent damage to the morals of the perpetrators. Abortion kills the conscience. Abortion enshrines murder. Abortion enthrones cowardice, selfishness, irresponsibility, immorality and lying. Abortion makes slaughter acceptable. By teaching us to dehumanize and devalue what we ought to prize and protect, abortion has unleashed a national epidemic of violence. Abortion teaches us that human life is cheap, disposable and expendable. *It is not!*

EVERY HUMAN LIFE IS A GIFT FROM GOD!

I renounce every demeaning, dehumanizing, degrading racist epithet. I do so, because God made all people in His image, and because Jesus loves all and chose to die for all: He paid the same immense price for all.

In the same spirit of love, I denounce every attempt to dehumanize, devalue and dismember the unborn child.

Uncommon sense sees that the slave and the baby are both precious people—not property—and that both have inalienable rights.

Uncommon sense sees that if black lives matter, then unborn lives matter, including the lives of black unborn babies.

Uncommon sense sees that if unborn lives don't matter, then no life matters.

Uncommon sense sees that *every single human life matters!*

No nation promoting abortion can survive as a free nation. It is doomed to fall—and it deserves to fall.

To be candid—and politically *incorrect*—abortion is our modern-day cover-up for our sexual immorality. Spouses commit adultery, single folk fornicate, the woman gets pregnant, and something must be done so that their immorality can continue without the baggage of an "unwanted child." "Free love" is not a "love revolution." "Free love" is lust; it is the exaltation of folly and self; it is the death of conscience. Lust is the counterfeit of love. As a nation, we have embraced and glamorized and made money off the counterfeit!

This is why the abortion doctor can speak with such calm, calculated ruthlessness about 'helping' the mother with her choice. It is the Nazi death-doctors all over again—but now our supposed profound 'gravitas' has been employed to gain societal acceptance of our 'compassionate' holocaust.

Abortion has killed America's soul—we now need a resurrection.

73

President Ronald Reagan wrote an essay on *Abortion and the Conscience of a Nation*, in which he said,

"We cannot diminish the value of one category of human life—the unborn—without diminishing the value of all human life."[57]

The atheistic elite want the freedom to pick and choose which individual lives have value. They begin with the unborn, but that is not where they intend to end. They intend to end *with you.*

Mother Teresa bravely spoke the truth at the 1994 Prayer Breakfast:

"the greatest destroyer of peace today is abortion, because it is a war against the child—a direct killing of the innocent child—murder by the mother herself. AND IF WE ACCEPT THAT A MOTHER CAN KILL HER OWN CHILD, HOW CAN WE TELL OTHER PEOPLE NOT TO KILL ONE ANOTHER? How do we persuade a woman not to have an abortion? As always, we must persuade her with love ... *Any country that accepts abortion is not teaching the people to love, but to use any violence to get what they want."*

How do these words strike you?

Do you agree?

If you do, watch out!

Today's atheistic elite are enraged when they hear such words, and they begin to plot against you when they see you nod your approval. Since you are pondering thoughts that *they* do not approve, you must be punished, silenced, thwarted, intimidated, bullied, attacked and suppressed.

74

---

[57] Ronald Reagan, *Abortion and the Conscience of the Nation*, Thomas Nelson Publishers, Nashville, TN, 1984, p. 18.

Since you are so 'arrogant' as to *dare* consider a worldview in utter contradiction to theirs, you are an enemy of the State, a godless State that has stopped being the enforcer of freedom, and has become the enforcer of political correctness.

Since you esteem the Bible as an absolute, authoritative and universal standard by which to judge not only personal morals but also the actions of the State, your existence can no longer be tolerated.

Since you dare to defy the atheistic elite, you must be harassed, hounded, reduced to poverty, and finally, killed. That is the devil's aim: *to change America into a godless nation where death reigns!*

The death of the unborn baby is the precursor to the death of freedom ... *and the death of you.*

I sound an alarm!

Atheistic-socialism does not value human life. The heartless are merciless and faithless and ruthless: they see human life as fecal matter. Their profanity exposes their evil heart.

People are precious—even the ones with syndromes.

In addition to the horrible holocaust of abortion, we have a grievous suicide rate and unspeakably gruesome mass shootings. All three are connected—and it takes *uncommon sense* to perceive the connection. Is your soul deeply disturbed by these things?

I suppose that if you can convince yourself that there is no God, then it is easy to convince yourself that the unborn baby is not a person: it is just non-viable 'fetal tissue.'

Uncommon sense sees that the atheist and the abortionist have been deprived of intelligence.

God asked Job,

"Did you give the beautiful wings to the peacocks? Or wings and feathers to the ostrich? Which leaves her eggs in the earth, and warms them in dust, and forgets that the foot may crush them, or that the wild beast may break them. *She is hardened against her young ones*, as though they were not hers: her labor (to lay eggs) is in vain without fear (she has no proper concern for their preservation); because *God has deprived her of wisdom, neither has He imparted to her understanding.*"[58]

While the peacock is the emblem of pride, the ostrich is the emblem of stupidity. The peacock struts. The ostrich has no natural affection. Most birds build nests in a safe place and there lay their eggs, to protect their young. The ostrich could care less about its young. The ostrich lays its eggs wherever, with no concern about what will happen to them.

Has America become an *Ostrich Nation?!*

Today's atheistic elite is fond of and infatuated with their own 'gravitas.' Abortion proves that their gravitas is folly. Atheism and hedonism reveal ostrich-level stupidity.

We may excuse the ostrich on the grounds that it is just an animal. What excuse do we have? Surely, we have more intelligence and *uncommon sense* than an ostrich! Or do we?

Human life is sacred. It is the gift of God.

Scripture is sacred. It is the Word of God.

Of course, the atheist has things that are sacred.

First, the 'fact' that he is god. Second, all his opinions. Third, abortion. To the atheist, abortion is the sacred right of all women: a right they fiercely insist upon above all others.

---

[58] Job 39:13-17

Now if someone claims the "right" to abort their baby, it is appropriate to demand, "Where did this right come from?"

Rights do not materialize out of nothing; rights must be granted by some authoritative source.

If the answer is, "The Supreme Court" then we have exalted government over God, we have made government greater than God, we have dethroned God from His rightful place as Creator and Judge and installed puppet emperors who die in His place.

The "right" to murder a baby is *not* found anywhere in our Constitution; it is only found in one place: *the wicked soul of the devil.*

The only source of inalienable rights is God Himself.

Our *Declaration of Independence* rings out:

"We hold these truths to be self-evident, that all men are *created* equal, that they are endowed *by their Creator* with certain unalienable Rights, that among these are *Life*, Liberty and the pursuit of Happiness."

Jefferson later wrote:

"God who gave us life gave us liberty. And can the liberties of a nation be thought secure when we have removed their only firm basis, a conviction in the minds of the people that *these liberties are the gift of God?"*[59]

President Kennedy, concurred, in his 1961 *Inaugural Address*, when he declared his unwavering commitment to the revolutionary belief, held by America's Founding Fathers, that "the rights of man come not from the generosity of the state *but from the hand of God.*"

77

[59] Federer, p. 323; from Jefferson's *Notes on the State of Virginia*, Query 18, 1781.

The *government* cannot grant inalienable rights: it can only recognize and uphold them. Only *God* can grant inalienable rights, and He most graciously has. If a government does not recognize and uphold our inalienable, God-given rights, then that government is illegitimate.

Christianity produces dignity of life and the sanctity of life. How? Because in the beginning when God created the universe, He said, *"Let us make man in our image."*[60] So then, people did not evolve from nothing over millions of years; people were intentionally made by God in the image of God. Therefore, human life is not on the same plane as animal life. However much we may value the lives of cats, cows and caterpillars, their life is not sacred. *But human life is!*

People with *uncommon sense* esteem the Bible. *Because they highly value the Bible, they highly value human life.* (The value you place on the Bible determines the value you place on human life. Think about that.)

The Bible gives us the best basis for respecting the life of the unborn. I paraphrase Psalm 139:13-15.

> *"For You have created my spirit, soul and body:*
> *You knit me together in my mother's womb.*
> *I will praise You; for I am fearfully*
> *and wonderfully made:*
> *I am Your unique workmanship:*
> *marvelous are Your works;*
> *this revelation penetrates deep in my soul.*
> *My body was not hid from You,*
> *when I was made in secret, and expertly wrought in the*
> *sanctuary of my mother's womb."*

In the Christian worldview, the mother's womb ought to be the ultimate sanctuary. Her womb ought to be the place of absolute safety.

78

---

[60] Genesis 1:26

In the atheistic worldview, the life of the baby (excuse me, 'the fetus') is irrelevant, even when it has been born. *Abortion will always lead to infanticide.* We are witnessing this gory, gut-wrenching tragedy right now. Those who embrace the atheistic worldview have no rational basis to restrict their own choices. Since they are god, they have absolute freedom to choose whatever they prefer. Conveniently, there is no God to whom they must answer.

Ethics divorced from God becomes the arbitrary will of the elite. Because it is arbitrary, it is fluid, changeable and subject to nothing. It is right simply because the elite say it is right. When men and women eliminate God, they become god, but death becomes king. When men and women divorce their reason from God's revelation, they can rationalize any behavior—no matter how vile, vicious or violent.

Under the Christian worldview, however, there is the strongest possible incentive to restrict our choices. Being *under God* means that God is not only our Maker, He is our Judge. There is a literal Judgment Day on which we will stand before God the Great Judge, who knows all and who sees all, and we will answer to Him for everything we said and did and why we did it—and be judged accordingly.

President Reagan wrote:

*"Abraham Lincoln recognized that we could not survive as a free land when some men could decide that others were not fit to be free and should therefore be slaves. Likewise, **we cannot survive as a free nation when some men decide that others are not fit to live and should be abandoned to abortion or infanticide.**"*[61]

Is there anyone who will rise up for God against liars and evildoers who see abortion as the supreme right of women?!

---

[61] Reagan, p. 38

Is there anyone who will reach out in mercy to the mother with an unexpected or unwanted pregnancy, and bring her the one thing that will save her and give her hope: Jesus?!

[Women of America! As a minister of reconciliation, I beg you: Come to Jesus, repent of your sin, and His powerful blood will remove the guilt of your sin and wash away your shame. Only do not listen to demons or to demonic wisdom!]

Let us weep because abortion is the triumph of a seared conscience—until our tears re-sensitize our conscience. Let us weep because our euphemisms cloak our sin. Let us weep because churches have compromised and endorsed abortion. Let us persevere in our stand for life until hearts are changed—until *"We, The People"* recognize the God-given value of every single human being. Quitting is not an option. Why? Because the sanctity of human life is non-negotiable. The truth is, abortion is worse than slavery: it is the equivalent of the Nazi death camps. Every abortion clinic is an Auschwitz, where babies are taken to die. Therefore:

Let abortion be banned!
Let eugenics be damned!
Let euthanasia and infanticide
be forever outlawed!

Change your heart, America! We must choose LIFE and kindness and compassion! We must NEVER choose to murder babies in the name of "reproductive freedom"! Women! With your uncommon sense, choose marriage and motherhood! Choose life! Men! With your uncommon sense, choose family and fatherhood! Choose life!

I believe that Americans will reject the demonic delusion of atheism, will renounce immorality, and will choose life instead of abortion. With all my heart I believe:

America will be saved!

8

MARRIAGE IS GOOD

Truth lies trampled in the streets ...
And the LORD saw it, and it displeased Him.[62]

If the foundations be destroyed,
what can the righteous do?[63]

Ethics must begin with the will of God. If God Almighty wills a particular behavior, then that behavior is ethical, right and good—for all. Arrogant atheists choke at this thought.

Let us be clear: if we foolishly deny God's existence and defy God's moral authority, then our ethics is nothing but a process of concoction under the influence of demons.

For example, marriage is the will of God.

Marriage is part of the foundation of a sound society.

What is marriage? Noah Webster gave this definition in his 1828 Dictionary:

---

[62] Isaiah 59:14,15
[63] Psalm 11:3

"Marriage: THE LEGAL UNION OF A MAN AND WOMAN FOR LIFE. Marriage is a contract both civil and religious, by which the parties engage to live together in mutual affection and fidelity, till death shall separate them. *Marriage was instituted by God Himself* for the purpose of preventing the promiscuous intercourse of the sexes, for promoting domestic felicity, and for securing the maintenance and education of children. *'Marriage is honorable in all and the bed undefiled.'* Heb. 13."

Perhaps you are surprised or unnerved to see a Bible verse embedded in a dictionary definition. But there it is.

God's Absolute Truth is the only proper foundation for our definitions.

For us to redefine marriage is national suicide.

In the beginning, when God created mankind, He made them male and female and instituted marriage: the union of one man and one woman.

Genesis is not religious fiction, mythology or philosophy. It is not in those inferior categories. No less an authority than the Lord Jesus Christ testified that *Genesis* is truth. Jesus said:

"Have ye not read, that He that made them at the beginning made them male and female, and said, For this cause shall a man leave father and mother, and shall cleave to his wife: and they two shall be one flesh?"[64]

If Jesus is mistaken about *Genesis*, then He cannot be trusted about anything. But in fact, Jesus was there in *Genesis*. He was personally present.

Jesus never began, but got the beginning started.

---

[64] Matthew 19:4-5

Jesus, with God the Father and God the Holy Spirit, spoke mankind into being, and made them, not male and male nor female and female, but male and female. Why? Male and male cannot produce children. Female and female cannot produce children.

It is God's will that a male be joined to a female—this is called monogamy. One man, one woman. Not one man and another man. No one man and multiple men. Not one man and multiple women. Not one woman and one woman. There are only two genders: male and female.

Marriage is not man's invention. Marriage was instituted by God for man's benefit. God gave us marriage for our good. *Marriage is the foundation of human civilization.* Any nation that does not honor and safeguard marriage is sowing seeds for its own obliteration. Strong marriages are the basis of strong families. Out of strong families come strong nations. Marriage portrays the mystery of the supernatural union between the Lord Jesus Christ and His Church. No wonder the devil seeks to denigrate marriage. When the United States legalized same-sex marriage, God did not amend or annul His own moral law.

Daniel foresaw the antichrist and pictured him as a horn, which is a symbol of his power:

"I beheld, and the same horn made war with the saints, and prevailed against them ... And he shall speak great words against the Most High, and shall wear out the saints of the Most High, and think to change times and laws." [65]

Why could he prevail against them and wear them out? Because they did not fast, pray, seek God's face and live right. *It is the work of the antichrist to attempt to change the fundamental laws of God.* Now you know the magnitude of what we are up against. Is all lost? No!

83

---

[65] Daniel 7:21,25

"But the people that do know their God (and not just know about Him) *shall be strong, and do exploits."*[66]

Before we can be strong, we must first be clean. Before we try to cast the speck out of the eyes of others, we must remove the log out of our own eyes. Before we condemn homosexual marriage and transgender insanity, we must first repent of all heterosexual sins: pornography, promiscuity, adultery, unscriptural divorce, sexual fantasies, and idolizing sex goddesses. Before we can use our spiritual authority over demons, we must rule over our own flesh. If our responsibility is to reclaim, restore and re-sensitize the conscience of America, then we must be pure as Jesus is pure.

Jesus never aims to damn sinners, but to deliver them. Jesus did not condemn the woman caught in adultery: He pardoned her and commanded her to sin no more. Jesus did not condemn the woman who had been married five times and was living with the sixth man: He freely offered her the water of life. Sinners need a Savior, and we are all sinners. Jesus alone gives us grace and truth, and He alone saves us from the guilt, shame, stain, power and penalties of our sin.

We must face facts. The sexual revolution is a celebration of immorality; it is defiance of the will of God; it is cheap sex masquerading as true love; and it is a door for demons to invade our nation and impose their nefarious will on us.

Today we must choose between the sweet duet of marital fidelity and the STD-strewn funeral dirge of sexual depravity. We must choose between the atheistic ethic of sex as a physical act between consenting adults, and the higher ethic of sex as a sacred, covenant act between husband and wife. When, by the grace of God, we choose holiness of heart and life:

America will be saved!

---

[66] Daniel 11:32

9

HOMOSEXUALITY

It is time for Thee, LORD, to work:
for they have made void Thy law.[67]

Sodom and Gomorrah,
and the cities about them in like manner,
giving themselves over to fornication, and going
after strange flesh, are set forth for an example,
suffering the vengeance of eternal fire ...
And on some have compassion, making a difference:
and others save with fear,
pulling them out of the fire;
hating even the garment spotted by the flesh.[68]

The hail shall sweep away the refuge of lies ...
Your covenant with death shall be cancelled.[69]

CAUTION: *Hail is about to fall!*

---

[67] Psalm 119:126
[68] Jude 1:7,22-23
[69] Isaiah 28:17-18

Truth is the basis of morality. God's Word is Truth: eternal Truth, *absolute* Truth, universal Truth! Holy Scripture alone gives us the authoritative basis for our perspective on homosexuality.

Meditate on Romans 1:18,24-28 (KJV text is in bold type).

1:18—**For the wrath,** the holy fury **of God is revealed from heaven against all ungodliness and unrighteousness of men, who hold** suppress and smother **the truth in unrighteousness** so they can spread their sin.

1:24—**Wherefore God also gave them up to uncleanness** homosexual perversion **through the lusts of their own hearts, to dishonor their own bodies between themselves:** *God gave them up* depicts His passive judgment against sinners; He lets them reap what they sow; He withdraws His restraining grace and lets the devil punish them. They sow sin, and reap incurable disease and premature death.

1:25—**Who changed** exchanged, corrupted **the truth of God into the lie** that they are god, **and worshipped and served the creature more** rather **than the Creator, who is blessed forever. Amen.**

Those who promote homosexuality and same-sex marriage are attempting to overturn the morals of God. Homosexuality is abomination in the sight of God. That is the politically incorrect but unchanging absolute truth of God.

1:26—**For this cause God gave them up unto vile** degrading **affections** passions: lesbianism, homosexuality: **for even their women did change the natural use into that which is against nature:**

Lesbianism and homosexuality are against nature.

It is a lie that God makes people homosexuals.

Think of cars in comparison to your body. You don't put gas in the exhaust pipe. The exhaust pipe is meant for elimination, not injection. Gas goes in the gas tank. Do I really need to spell out the illustration? The design of God means that our anus was meant for elimination.

1:27—And likewise also the men, leaving the natural God-ordained **use of** relations with **the woman, burned in their lust one toward another; men with men working that which is unseemly** shameless and indecent acts, **and receiving in themselves that recompence** just penalty **of their error which was meet:** it is the devil who rewards sinners with disease; God rewards believers with eternal life.

1:28—And even as they did not like to retain God in their knowledge: because they considered God worthless (His truth is not to their taste)**, God gave them over to a reprobate** worthless **mind:** so void of *uncommon sense* that it applauds sin and attacks holiness **to do those things which are not convenient:** self-destructive and horrid things that should never be done.

A reprobate mind is a mind so depraved that it embraces the vilest abominations.

My godly friends: May you never cease to shudder with repulsion at what reprobate minds rationalize, defend and try to force on the rest of us. But having said this, we must hasten to add:

Jesus does not hate homosexuals: He loves them.

Jesus does not give homosexuals AIDS.

Jesus took AIDS on Himself, along with every other sickness that curses mankind, and *with His stripes we are healed.*[70]

---

[70] Isaiah 53:5

Jesus is not the Author of death. Jesus is the Author of life. Jesus does not send people to hell; people choose hell when they choose sin.

Jesus is not against men having bonds of friendship with men; He is against what dishonors the body and destroys the soul.

THE LAWS OF NATURE AND NATURE'S GOD

Our Lord Jesus Christ made moral laws as well as natural laws. He made a moral universe, a universe that punishes sin and rewards holiness. The moral law springs from the holy nature of God and is designed for our good.

Think first of the natural laws of our universe, all of which have consequences. There is the law of gravity. There are the laws of electricity, the laws of physics, and so forth. The law of seedtime and harvest comes to mind: What we sow, we reap.

We cannot change these natural laws, but God gave us brains and *common sense* so that we would work them for our advantage.

God also made substances to bless us. For example, God made plants—such as tobacco—but not to the intent that we smoke it. He expects us to use our *common sense* so that substances help us, rather than enslave us.

Now take the issue of sex.

The world refers to 'unprotected sex'—proof that sex with anyone anytime anywhere can lead to terrible consequences: incurable sexually transmitted diseases, as well as 'unwanted pregnancies.' Those STDs are warning signs that we are not using sex as the Designer intended.

Our bodies were not made for immorality of any kind, but for the Lord. This is the unchangeable moral law of the living God.

We cannot repeal God's moral laws, but by God's almighty grace we can choose to operate them for our benefit, and to do so is *uncommon sense.*

The renewed mind delights in the moral law of God.

The reprobate mind despises the moral law of God.

God made marriage, and He made marriage to be between one man and one woman—a lifelong union.

The atheistic elite think it a sign of their uber-intelligence to attack and reverse God's moral laws, but when they do, they unleash powers of destruction against society.

MY PERSONAL WORD TO HOMOSEXUALS

If you are a homosexual, I love you. I respect you: but I do not agree with your behavior. I value you enough to tell you the truth, truth you may not like, at first. Mercy without truth is not love.

If I tell you that God has redefined right and wrong, I would be a cowardly liar. If I tell you that God now accepts what He used to find abominable, I would be lying to your face.

Will I love you? Yes.

Lie to you? No.

Tell you half-truths? No.

Affirm your worth as a human being? Yes.

Accept your lifestyle? No.

Tolerate your sin? No.

Esteem you as one for whom Jesus died? Yes.

Buy your rationalizations? No.

Use homophobic slurs to mock you? No.

Speak the truth in love to you? Yes. Always.

I do not judge you: *I am not better than you. I need a Savior, just like you. I need great mercy, too. I need sweet freedom from the deception and shackles of sin, too.*

The love of God for you compels me to say this to you:

- To rationalize sin is to deceive yourself.
- To defend sin is to delude yourself.
- To promote sin is to damn yourself.

I do not want you to be deceived, deluded or damned!

Jesus did not come to earth to condemn you, but to die for you and to give you the gift of eternal life. *That* is true love!

Jesus did not come to *shame* sinners but to *save* sinners.

Jesus loves us not by redefining sin or accepting our sin, and not by ignoring our sin, but by giving us freedom from our sin, from its guilt, its shame, its misery, its awful curse, its heavy chain! *That* is genuine love!

My friend, if you repent and receive Jesus as your Lord, He will bring His supernatural blessing into your life! *That's what I want for you!* One day, an eager car salesman told me that a certain upcoming car model was to die for. I thought about that. No car is to die for. But *you* are to die for. Jesus thinks so. Jesus actually did die for you. Why? Because He loves you. Why did He need to die for you? Because if He didn't, you would have to pay the penalty for your sin. The penalty for sin is not just physical death, but hell and the lake of fire. Jesus does not want that for you. I don't, either. I do not want you to damn yourself. I do not want you to suffer endless incarceration with unlimited torment.

If you go to hell, it will not be because Jesus
does not love you—but because you spurned His love.
If you go to hell, it will not be because you had to go there,
but because you chose to cling to your sin and your pride.

Jesus did not make hell for humans, but for demons. Jesus warned us that hell is real, that hell is unbearably hot, that hell is a prison of torment from which there is no escape. In hell, Jesus revealed, the unrepentant, uncaring, narcissistic rich man cried out: *"I am tormented in this flame!"*[71] God does not want you eternally tormented: but you have to choose to receive His love. God is not your enemy. God does not conquer you by force. God wins you by love. Try to find another supposed-savior who died for you. There isn't one. *Only Jesus* loved you enough to die for you. Only Jesus rose from the dead to die no more. Only Jesus! Today His arms are stretched wide open *toward you!* God's power does not govern what He does: His love does. He loves you and wants you to spend eternity with Him in heaven. What is the way to heaven? JESUS. You need Jesus.

Truth is not a man-made philosophy.

Truth is an eternal Person.

Arguing about God accomplishes nothing. *You can debate until you die. But you can encounter Jesus today, as Lord and God, and be changed. That's what I want for you!!!*

TRUTH FOR CHURCHES

The following is going to be stern, but it needs to be.

Churches that approve same-sex marriage have betrayed the Savior. Churches that ordain homosexuals have stabbed the Savior in His back. Churches that promote homosexuality twist Scripture to their own damnation. You apostates that defy the morals of God: *Repent of your treachery!*

I have a message from God for you:

"You know this: No whoremonger, *nor unclean person,* nor covetous man, who is an idolater, has any inheritance in the kingdom of Christ and of God."

91

---

[71] Luke 16:24; read the entire story about hell: Luke 16:19-31

"Know ye not that the unrighteous shall not inherit the kingdom of God? Be not deceived: neither fornicators, nor idolaters, nor adulterers, *nor effeminate, nor abusers of themselves with mankind,* nor thieves, nor covetous, nor drunkards, nor revilers, nor extortioners, shall inherit the kingdom of God."

"Now the works of the flesh are manifest, which are these: Adultery, fornication, *uncleanness,* lasciviousness, idolatry, witchcraft, hatred, variance, emulations, wrath, strife, seditions, heresies, envyings, murders, drunkenness, revellings, and such like: of the which I tell you before, as I have also told you in time past, that they which do such things shall not inherit the kingdom of God."

"Knowing this, that the law is not made for a righteous man, but for the lawless and disobedient, for the ungodly and for sinners, for unholy and profane, for murderers of fathers and murderers of mothers, for manslayers, for whoremongers, *for them that defile themselves with mankind,* for menstealers, for liars, for perjured persons, and if there be any other thing that is contrary to sound doctrine."[72]

If you are wondering what behavior God disapproves, reread these verses. God has drawn a line. He gives you grace not to cross it, mercy when you do, and unfailing love to keep you on the straight and narrow road to everlasting life!

Jesus did not preach acceptance of abomination; He preached deliverance to the captives!

May we never twist Scripture or pervert the grace of God to justify demonic perversions. Let us glorify God with our bodies. Let us pursue holiness in the fear of God, knowing that then:

America will be saved!

---

[72] Ephesians 5:5; 1 Corinthians 6:9-10; Galatians 5:19-21; 1 Timothy 1:9-10; research Revelation 21:8; 22:15.

10

ALL
Lives Matter

**I permit no man to narrow and degrade
my soul by making me hate him.**
—Booker Taliaferro Washington

I HAVE A DREAM
that my four children will one day live in a nation
where they will not be judged by the color
of their skin but by the content of their character.
—Dr. Martin Luther King, Jr.

All things whosoever ye would that men
should do to you, do ye even so to them.[73]
—the Lord Jesus Christ (the Golden Rule)

Jesus is the Ultimate Reconciler. The Blood of Jesus destroys the
sham of superiority and forever establishes the worth, the value and
the dignity of every human being.

93

---

[73] Matthew 7:12

To my African-American friends: God has made of one blood all races, so there is really only one race: The God-made human race.

Racism, white supremacy, the KKK, police brutality and injustice have no place in America.

I refuse to let anyone or any devil divide us. Atheistic political correctness cannot eliminate racism or bring healing, but Jesus can. By the wisdom of Jesus, we can achieve social justice. By the Blood of Jesus, we can achieve racial reconciliation. By the love of Jesus governing our lives, we can exterminate the scourge of racism and build a better future. Nothing less than the Blood of the Son of God can take away the guilt, the agony and the injustice of murder and produce healing. This is why I lift up Jesus.

The Civil Rights movement changed America because it was led by a preacher who had the *uncommon sense* to know the difference between non-violent protests, and rioting, retaliation and retribution. Dr. King saw a better way than "an eye for an eye." As he sat in prison in the spring of 1963, he wrote *"Letter from Birmingham Jail"* which is still pertinent today:

"Was not Jesus an extremist for love: "Love your enemies, bless them that curse you, do good to them that hate you, and pray for them which despitefully use you, and persecute you.' ... the question is not whether we will be extremists, but what kind of extremists we will be. *Will we be extremists for hate or for love?"[74]*

Political correctness will never create extremists for love because it is man-made control from the outside that leaves the inside unchanged. The love of Jesus changes us from the inside. His love is a supernatural power, a living reality that changes how we see God, and others and ourselves. Only His love governing our hearts can turn racism into reconciliation.

94

[74] Dr. Martin Luther King Jr., *I Have a Dream: Writings and Speeches that Changed the World*, HarperCollins Publisher, San Francisco, CA, 1986,1992, p.94.

When I think about what your race has suffered for over 400 years, I am stunned by the undeniable record of gross hypocrisy, vicious hostility and savage injustice. Only Jesus knows the depth of your pain.

Murder must be met with judgment—not by individual revenge or lawless looting, but by the swift hand of government. But justice alone does not satisfy the heart—either the heart of the victimized or the heart of God. Under the old covenant, there was no animal sacrifice for murder because the blood of animals was in no way comparable to the worth of a person. When Jesus bore our sin, He satisfied both the justice of God and the love of God, and made possible reconciliation between God and man, and all people groups. Only the Blood of Jesus can cleanse the blood of murder. Only the love of Jesus can free us from the chains of hatred. His love *for* us can flow *through* us. That is what makes healing happen. It is not easy to love or forgive when we are hated. It is not just not easy—it is impossible. But Jesus makes the impossible possible by infusing our hearts with His love and grace. Only Jesus does that.

Booker T. Washington (1856-1915), whose life displayed the triumph of God's love and grace, wrote:

"Great men cultivate love ... only little men cherish a spirit of hatred ... With God's help, I have completely rid myself of any ill feeling toward the Southern white man for any wrong he inflicted upon my race."

This man of God understood that racist efforts to thwart the black vote caused permanent injury to the morals of the white folk involved; he also knew that *all* whites were *not* inherently racist, that thousands had fought to end slavery, and that many were committed to the elevation of the black race—proved by their gladly giving money to the Tuskegee Institute he founded.[75]

95

---

[75] Booker T. Washington, *Up From Slavery*, Penguin Books, Penguin Putnam Inc., New York, New York, 1986, pp. 165-166, 193.

Racism is not systemic in America: equality is.

Hatred is not systemic in America: freedom is.

Injustice is not systemic in America: Truth is.

The Truth is: ALL black lives matter. *Including black Republicans.* No *white* man can tell you that you *ain't black* because you don't vote for the Democrat Party. No *white* man can define your blackness. Your blackness is a gift from Almighty God. ALL black lives matter. *Including black policemen and policewomen* who bravely serve on our law enforcement teams and help save black lives. ALL black lives matter. *Including unborn black babies* that would be aborted by greedy white abortionists. ALL black lives matter. *Including black gang members* who have been given the poison-laced gift of atheistic education that leaves them vulnerable to the unscrupulous. ALL black lives matter. *Including blacks* in our inner cities whose murders go unreported by the lying media.

Let every white person boldly declare: *ALL black lives matter.* Let every black person reply: *ALL white lives matter.* Together let us raise a mighty chorus that drowns out the angry voices of division: *ALL LIVES MATTER. All lives no matter their racial mix matter. **All lives matter!!!***

I reaffirm: ALL black lives matter—and that slaps Marxist philosophy in the face. Karl Marx was a racist, an enemy of righteousness, a child of the devil, and he poisoned the world with Marxism.[76]

Marxism is the opiate of the people.

Let everyone know: Marxism is anti-Truth, anti-Freedom and anti-American. Marxism is a demonic counterfeit, a godless philosophy that creates misery and hell on earth; it is demonic wisdom. Marxism is a liar: it promises to eliminate income inequality but strips away income-producing opportunity.

---

[76] Read Richard Wurmbrand, *Marx & Satan; see the next chapter.*

Marxism destroys the creation of wealth by mandating incentive-killing regulations.

Marxism gives birth to socialism and communism—and both form a future that you don't want to be part of.

Forced redistribution of wealth is Marxism—and it is a counterfeit remedy for injustice and inequality. Forced redistribution of wealth cannot atone for the sins of yesteryear. Forced redistribution of wealth cannot satisfy man's insatiable thirst for revenge.

Marxism brings redistribution of wealth, all right, to the ultra-rich—but not to you.

Incentivized creation of wealth is distinctly American—and it is God's way to lift us all out of poverty.

Poverty is inherent in Marxism. Societal dysfunction is inherent in Marxism. The disintegration of the family is inherent in Marxism. Hatred of God is inherent in Marxism. Lying is inherent in Marxism. Marx spoke of a classless society; it was a straight-up lie. *There is one class in Marxism: the ruling class. If you're not in that privileged class, woe to you!*

Marx is not the way.

JESUS is the way.

Marxism is a dead-end.

JESUS is the Way, the Truth, and the Life.

God made us out of one blood, the blood of Adam, and redeemed us by one blood: the blood of Jesus. The remedy for greed and injustice is not the lies of Marxism, socialism or communism—but the love of Jesus. Hatred, violence and lies will not lead us to a better America: they will destroy America. We need to listen again to voices of heavenly wisdom.

Anointed by God, Dr. King trumpeted trenchant words in front of the Lincoln Memorial in the summer of 1963:

"I HAVE A DREAM that one day this nation will rise up and live out the true meaning of its creed: 'We hold these truths to be self-evident, that all men are created equal.'"

Man cannot bestow equality. Equality is the gift of God, proved by *the* Gift of His Son, Jesus Christ, who died for *all.*

"I HAVE A DREAM that one day on the red hills of Georgia, the sons of former slaves and the sons of former slave owners will be able to sit down together at the table of brotherhood."

Without morality rooted in genuine Christianity, there will be no table of brotherhood.

"I HAVE A DREAM that one day even the state of Mississippi, a state sweltering with the heat of injustice, sweltering with the heat of oppression, will be transformed into an oasis of freedom and justice."

Without God's grace, no human heart, born in sin, raised in racism and saturated with lies, can ever be transformed.

"I HAVE A DREAM that my four little children will one day live in a nation where they will not be judged by the color of their skin but by the content of their character."

Without the love of Jesus, no one will have character and all our judgments will be external and miserably flawed. It is His love filling and pouring through our hearts that will destroy racism and prevent the spread of hostility.

"I HAVE A DREAM that one day every valley shall be exalted, and every hill and mountain shall be made low, the rough places will be made plain, and the crooked places will be made straight; 'and the glory of the Lord shall be revealed and all flesh shall see it together.'"[77]

Without Great Awakening, all this will be a vanished dream. But I have faith that America will be saved *through you!*

I have a dream that you, my African-American friends, will receive the love of Jesus and will spread His love to all.; that you will lead our nation back to righteousness and the right use of freedom, that you will stand up without fear or compromise for God's everlasting truth.

I have a dream that you will emphatically reject the seduction of same-sex marriage, recognizing that sexual behavior is a choice, not comparable at all to the civil rights which your race struggled so righteously and so long to gain.

I have a dream that you will spurn the pseudo-education forced on you by atheists, an evolution-based system that is inherently racist and unscientific, and will take the lead in creating curriculum worth learning: curriculum grounded in God's Truth that will empower our young people to develop their God-given abilities and teach them to value all people.

I have a dream that because of your influence, all people will recognize that every human life is the gift of God and ought to be cherished and protected from the moment of conception. Because of the soul-stabbing saga of slavery and segregation that you and your forefathers suffered, you have a perspective that uniquely equips you to reject the dehumanizing lie that the fetus is sub-human tissue that the mother-master can dispose of as she sees fit.

---

[77] King, p. 104

I prophesy: With your help, abortion will go the way of slavery!

You should know that a white supremacist gave you *Planned Parenthood* [as if black babies don't matter—*all* black lives matter!]; that white atheists gave you a godless and broken system of "education"; that white atheists gave you drugs: cocaine and heroin. Those "gifts" are laced with poison, and they are designed to put us all on the government plantation and reduce us all to enslaved nobodies that the "elite" can dictate to or dispose of as they see fit.

This essay is not about any political party or your own party affiliation. Perhaps it is time for you to form a new political party and leverage your clout. No political party has a right to your vote.

In any case, do not be silent and do not be silenced. Do not sacrifice your God-given voice and vote for measly crumbs dished out by a socialist slave master intoxicated with his own self-indulging wisdom! What we need is Jesus, and He is not a socialist. We must love Him and honor Him *above any political party.* We must also replace loyalty to a political party with loyalty to godly and wise principles. We must know what each party stands for, what each candidate stands for, and support and vote for only those who stand up for our *American* principles of freedom, justice for all and righteousness *under God.*

Let *every* American be *independent* in their thinking, devoutly and defiantly committed to the Bible, and loyal to our *Declaration of Independence* and our Constitution, and especially the Bill of Rights. Blind loyalty to any political party blinds us to what we really need: the wisdom of God and the blessing of God. We must also have the love and grace of God.

For you to lead, you will have to draw from a different well than secular humanism. The well I am speaking of is actually the secret source of our *Declaration of Independence.*

What is that secret source? I'll give you a clue: What *one* book did your forefathers want to read before they died? ...

The B – I – B – L – E. The Bible.

The God of the Bible who emancipated Israel from slavery in Egypt is the God referenced in our *Declaration*.

Our *Declaration of Independence* is a profoundly spiritual document that flows out of something different than atheistic 'enlightenment.'

Let me be blunt. If we are evolved from nothing, then the *Declaration of Independence* is a lie and America is built on a colossal lie.

Today, some like to describe themselves as "progressives" who move forward. But this is smooth talk disguising atheistic ideology. What the *Declaration of Independence* stated so eloquently cannot be improved upon, because Truth cannot be improved. Truth is. To depart from Truth is to go backwards, not forwards. Either all of us are created equal by our Creator, or we go backwards to the horrific centuries when there was no equality. Either we all are endowed with inalienable rights by our Creator, either the government derives its just powers from the consent of the governed, or we go backwards to the Dark Ages when elitists dished out crumbs and restricted rights and liberties at their whim.

In order for you, my African-American friends, to fulfill your destiny *under God*, you must esteem the same source that the first freedom-loving Americans knew, and intentionally drink from that sacred well.

God gave us this Book—not to swell our heads—but to transform our hearts. God gave us *His* Book to lead us to *Him*. God gave us the Bible to empower us to change what needs to be changed in our communities and our nation. To censor this Book or leave it to collect dust, is to leave our children defenseless before the enemies of freedom and of God.

The timeless principles enshrined in our *Declaration of Independence* came from the Bible. Think of the Bible as the root system for the Tree of Liberty. To neglect or reject the Bible is to cause the Tree to wither. We cannot enjoy the fruit of freedom if we destroy the roots of righteousness *under God*. A tree cannot grow apart from the roots from which it sprang.

In the Name of Jesus, I challenge you read the Bible daily. Feed on it; study it diligently; meditate on it; marinate your soul in its truths; put into practice what you read; do what God commands you to do. Let your home be a place where the Bible is respected, honored and obeyed. Then—your best days lie ahead.

Then, *you* will be the ones who declare: *"All lives matter because of Jesus."* Do black lives matter? Yes. *All* of them.

I stand with you: why not stand with me for unity *under God*, locking arms with me to protest and defy demonic division the next time we sing our National Anthem?

Learn your history from unbiased sources, including the hearts of faith that changed it. The heroes of your heritage were Christians. They loved God! They loved the Bible! To them, the Bible was the source of life, an anchor of hope, and the *Declaration of Independence* was also a beacon of hope. They trusted in the living God and that trust fueled their unquenchable desire for liberty, equality and opportunity. Their strong confidence in God was the indispensable secret of their spectacular endurance and their impact on this world. May you, their heirs, follow their footsteps of faith and then go make your mark on history as they did, for the glory of God! Eternal vigilance is the price we must all pay to obtain and maintain liberty and justice for all and for our posterity. Without you, America cannot be saved. *But with you, with your uncommon sense and uncommon faith:*

America will be saved!

11

MARXISM CANCELLED

**Evil men and seducers shall wax worse and worse,
deceiving and being deceived.**[78]

**Now the Holy Spirit reveals plainly,
that in the latter times
one after another shall depart from the faith,
giving heed to seducing spirits,
and devil-inspired doctrines.**[79]

**And many false prophets shall arise,
and shall deceive many. And because anarchy
shall abound, the love of many shall wax cold ...
And this Gospel of the Kingdom shall be preached
in all the world for a witness unto all nations;
and then shall the end come.**
—the Lord Jesus Christ[80]

---

[78] 2 Timothy 3:13
[79] 1 Timothy 4:1
[80] Matthew 24:11,2,14

If anything *deserves* to be cancelled, it is Marxism. If anything *should* be cancelled, it is Marxism. If anything *must* be cancelled, it is Marxism. Every American needs to understand why Marxism is a devil-inspired doctrine and what is required to reduce it to a despised, dead relic.

Secular conservativism cannot cancel Marxism; it has no cancelling power. The only thing that will cancel the curse of Marxism is the Gospel of Jesus Christ. This is why Marxists hate the Bible: they are scared of it, and so is the devil.

Marxism is the opiate of the people. Jesus is Living Bread. Marxism is a mirage. Jesus is an oasis. Marxism is a category five hurricane spinning off tornadoes. Jesus is a spectacular sunrise. Marxism is a wolf. Jesus is the Lion of Judah. Only the roar of *this* risen Lion will make the Marxist wolf shrink back.

Marxism is named after Karl Marx (1818-1883). The most famous writing of Marx is the *Communist Manifesto,* an essay he and Engels wrote in 1848. Marx began,

> *"The history of all hitherto existing society is the history of class struggles ... oppressor and oppressed."*

To use Marx's terminology, the oppressor is *"the bourgeoisie"* and the oppressed are *"the proletarians"*—the oppressors are capitalists and the oppressed are the workers. This is all rubbish.

The history of mankind is the history of God's salvation, delivering all people from the oppression of the devil.

The devil is the Oppressor. Jesus is the Deliverer. The devil works to divide and conquer. The devil wants to divide humanity against itself so we hate each other and fight each other and try to conquer each other (while demons snicker in scorn, unseen). According to Marx, the oppressors are evil: they must be exterminated, and the oppressed have a right to destroy their oppressors. This is inhumane ideology.

Jesus has a better way: the oppressors must be born again. The oppressors must be filled with the Holy Spirit and governed by the love of God, so that they voluntarily use their wealth to lift others and empower others. Grace changes greed into giving.

What about the oppressed? The oppressed must be born again. The oppressed must be filled with the Holy Spirit and governed by the love of God, so that they love their enemies and by so doing rise above their wickedness and folly, and then create new wealth by the wisdom of God.

Jesus is into the creation of wealth and the voluntary, compassionate giving of wealth to bless others. Jesus is not into the hoarding of wealth, the stealing of wealth, the destroying of wealth, or the government-mandated redistribution of wealth. The power to generate wealth is His gift.

Marx demanded the abolition of three things: (1) private property (2) the family and (3) Christianity. This is the height of folly. We need all three! To abolish these three is to abolish a fourth: *freedom*. Marxism has the exact wrong remedy for society's ills.

Private property is a safeguard against the overreach of would-be dictators. *The family*—the father + mother family—is a bulwark against misguided zealots promoting a one world government. *Christianity*—the dynamic relationship with God every person can have through the Lordship of Jesus and the indwelling Holy Spirit—is the stumbling block to all tyrants.

Marx wrote,

"the first step in the revolution by the working class is to raise the proletariat to the position of ruling class ... this cannot be effected except by means of DESPOTIC inroads on the rights of property, and on the conditions of bourgeois production.

But when does this despotism end? In practice, *never*.

What Marx gave us is one despotism triumphing over a different despotism. The despotism of the proletariat is no more benevolent than the despotism of the bourgeoisie. What good does it do to replace one godless ruling class with a different godless ruling class? Both feature power over the people and power to the state—therefore, disregard their polished rhetoric that says the opposite: "power to the people."

Now here is a key thought: whatever Marx said is true, is a lie. For example, *"The proletarians have nothing to lose but their chains."* No—they can lose their lives and their immortal souls and their eternal rewards. Here is the full quote, at the conclusion of the *Manifesto*:

> *"The Communists disdain to conceal their views and aims. They openly declare that their ends can be attained only by THE FORCIBLE OVERTHROW of all existing social conditions. Let the ruling classes tremble at a Communistic revolution. The proletarians have nothing to lose but their chains. They have a world to win. Working Men of All Countries, Unite!"*

Workers have nothing to lose but their chains? Not so! They will lose their immortal souls, if they listen to Marx. He who trades his soul for money is ignorant of the value of his own soul.

Jesus asked, *"What does it profit a man if he gains the whole world and loses his soul?"*[81]

No amount of gold equals the value of your soul. Money does not make life worthwhile: God does. Will oppressed workers lose anything else if they listen to Marx? Emphatically, yes; tragically, yes! They will lose the sparkle in their eye, they will lose their incentive to create, they will lose their God-given purpose, they will lose their reason for being and their will to live, and they will mope in unbearably heavy, invisible chains forged by the government-god that is over them, dictating their every move.

---

[81] Matthew 16:26

Americans! Marx fixated on income inequality.

Jesus gives you a better equality: equality with Himself.

Income inequality is inevitable; injustice is not. Justice begins with the fear of God, the Ultimate Judge. What we Americans value is equality of opportunity. There will always be inequalities in income, because some are more gifted than others, some are more diligent than others, and some have a head start from their parents more than others. But if we provide freedom under law along with equal opportunity, then any individual can soar to the height of his or her God-given destiny. That is part of what makes America attractive: it is freedom without anarchy, and opportunity without injustice.

With accurate knowledge of the past 120 years, in which more than 120 million innocent people have been slaughtered by Marxist regimes, we ought to be able to discern Marx' bottom line. His real aim was not to win the world but to wreck it. His goal was not to lift humanity into utopia, but to kick humanity into the bottomless pit. Marx did not care about either the oppressor or the oppressed—they are both expendable pawns in his war against God's supremacy. For Marx, it was immaterial who is in the privileged ruling class; he wanted despotism and a diabolical despot destroying everything.

Richard Wurmbrand, who suffered the horrors of Marxism under the freedom-crushing Communist regime in Romania, exposed the evil heart of Marx in his book, *Marx & Satan*. Marx wrote a poem called *"The Player"* which has these lines:

"The hellish vapors rise and fill the brain
Till I go mad and my heart is utterly changed.
See this sword? The prince of darkness sold it to me.
For me he beats the time and gives the signs.
Ever more boldly I play the dance of death."[82]

[82] Richard Wurmbrand, *Marx & Satan*, Living Sacrifice Book Company, Bartlesville, OK, 1986, p. 15.

That is what Marxism is, a demon-inspired dance of death.

Marx also wrote a drama entitled *"Oulanem"* which has these lines:

"Yet I have power within my youthful arms
To clench and crush you with tempestuous force
While for us both the abyss yawns in darkness.
You will sink down and I shall follow laughing,
Whispering in your hears, 'Descend, come with me, friend.'"[83]

Where does Marxism lead? To one place: the abyss. Marxism morphs the government into a monster with an insatiable appetite for power and control, into a cruel slave-master with an unappeasable appetite for your money and your freedom, and into a micro-managing bully that tells you how high to jump.

No matter what you call it, Marxism, Communism, Socialism, Progressivism, Liberalism—it's all the same thing in essence. Re-imagine it and re-name it whatever a slick politician or think-tank conjures up—even "New-Americanism"—it is the same old *anti-*American *un-*American deception.

It is insufficient to try to combat Marxism by conservative capitalist policies alone, or with character classes that delete Christ and the Bible. To do so is to misunderstand and underestimate Marx and Marxism. It is the equivalent of charging hell with a water pistol.

Marxism is demonic; it is supernatural seduction. Therefore, it can be overcome only be those who know the One who beat death: JESUS CHRIST. If you know Him, then you can join me and cancel Marxism. And that will assuredly happen, because:

America will be saved!

---

[83] Ibid., p. 16

12

SUM IT UP: *CONTROL* IS THE *REAL* ISSUE

**I call heaven and earth to record this day against you,
that I have set before you, life and death,
blessing and cursing: Therefore, *choose life*,
that both you and your seed may live.**[84]

The main issue to today's atheistic elite is control. They want to be in control and they want to control you. They want all power, and they want to take away your freedom, your money and all your power. If that alarms you, your *uncommon sense* is working!

Today's atheistic elite are attempting to pull off a total overthrow of God's moral order—and then to force an ungodly, un-American new world order on you. They aim to force three things on us: atheism, socialism and perversion. Their goal is to undo America's identity and undermine America's destiny by untying America from God. They want you to think that freedom means that no one—not even God Himself—can tell you what to do. This spurious definition of freedom is the doorway to hell.

---

[84] Deuteronomy 30:19

Real freedom is the ability to obey God in everything, without government interference or retaliation. God does not force us to obey Him: those with *uncommon sense* choose to obey Him because they see that He loves us with true love. They see that His moral commandments keep us from self-destruction.

In order to develop *uncommon sense*, you cannot listen to atheistic nonsense. Rather, you must listen to God: you must read His Word and listen to men and women of God, daily.

Today's atheistic elite want you to believe that abortion is not murder: that it is a mother's sacred right. They want you to believe that homosexuality is not a crime against nature and against God, but is perfectly normal. They want you to follow them absolutely, without questioning them. Should they consider infanticide a right, or euthanasia, or prostitution or polygamy or pedophilia or bestiality— you are not to think a thought contrary or say a word in contradiction.

If you see that freedom from God's reality and holy morality is really slavery to a power-drunk, lying, wicked elite, your *uncommon sense* is working!

Today's atheistic elite want you to believe that the government will give you everything for nothing—for free! They seduce you through the offers of free health care and free college—not telling you that you will be taxed into poverty. They want you to trust *them* to know what is best for you in every area of your life! They want you to rely on them, that is, on the State, from the cradle to the grave.

If the prospect of atheists running every detail of your life nauseates you, your *uncommon sense* is working!

Today's atheistic elite tout their *tolerance*. In fact, they are intolerant of Christianity and of Christians who have a spine.

Today's atheistic elite brag of their *inclusion*. In fact, they exclude any who dare to say different.

Today's atheistic elite boast of their *diversity*. In fact, they demand uniformity of thought and conformity to political correctness (however they define that).

If you see through their 3-fold lie of tolerance, inclusion and diversity, your *uncommon sense* is working!

Today's atheistic elite demand that America change its gods: they want America to divorce the living God who is the Fountain of living waters, and marry the demon god of atheistic socialism.

Make no mistake: atheistic socialism is a broken cistern that cannot possibly preserve the blessings of liberty and prosperity. The 'anything-goes' perversion of atheism is a recipe for one thing: national disaster.

Is your *uncommon sense* kicking in yet?

Atheism would make Americans unthinking slaves of the god-state. Those with *uncommon sense* take warning.

To be independent of controlling government, *"We, the People"* must declare our dependence on the living God, because only those who depend on God for protection and provision will have the courage to stand up to atheistic control freaks, and the morality to ensure that their liberty will not end in vice and violence.

The Psalmist did not declare, "My help comes from government entitlement programs." No! With his *uncommon faith he declared:*

"My help comes from the LORD, who made heaven and earth ... The LORD is thy keeper: the LORD is thy shade upon thy right hand ... The LORD shall preserve thee from all evil: He shall preserve thy soul. The LORD shall preserve thy going out and thy coming in from this time forth, and even for evermore."[85]

---

[85] Psalm 121:2,5,7,8

To look to government to solve all our problems is to make government god. Government was never meant to be the source of your supply, the answer to all your problems. *Government must never take the place of God.*

Government-as-god cannot create prosperity; instead it spreads poverty under the guise of redistributing wealth!

Uncommon sense recognizes these realities:

(1) Truth is the foundation of liberty and morality. Not, "*my* truth" or "*your* truth"—but *God's eternal absolute Truth.*

(2) Ethics must be based on two facts: there is a God, and, man is not god. Ethics that deny these facts cannot produce morality or maintain "the land of the free."

(3) Freedom cannot survive without moral foundations. Morality cannot survive without the Christian worldview.

(4) Government is not god.

I reiterate:

- **YOU ARE NOT GOD.**
- **GOVERNMENT IS NOT GOD.**

Five things are inseparable: Truth, Christianity, morality, liberty and prosperity.

These five things are likewise inseparable: lies, atheism, immorality, government-as-god and poverty.

We must all wise up to what the devil has in mind for our nation—and for every nation, for that matter. The devil's only aim is to steal, kill and destroy. Jesus said so, and Jesus cannot lie. The devil works by deceiving. He is a liar. But he is also a loser. He couldn't keep Jesus dead.

Understand that the devil and his demons influence people's minds. It is obvious to me that ling, unclean, and vicious demons inspired Lenin and Stalin and Marx and Nietzsche and Hitler. Their ideas came from hell—but millions bought into them, and brought untold millions to premature graves.

I wrote earlier about cruel compassion. *Cruel compassion* is an oxymoron, but blatant contradictions do not bother today's atheistic elite. All that matters to them is that they are recognized as god and that their opinions are esteemed and applauded as god-like pronouncements, whether or not they change every few months or years.

The only thing ultimately sacred to the atheist is that he is god. As god, whatever he wants to do will be considered right.

To the atheistic elite, nothing is right or wrong in a final sense. Morality and truth are inherently fluid; they are no longer inherently fixed. What is wrong today may be right tomorrow. What is true today may be untrue and worthy of death tomorrow.

Ancient Greek philosophers used to idolize "the true, the good, and the beautiful." But Jesus Christ does not deal in abstract philosophy. He deals with everyday reality.

For today's atheistic elite, truth is whatever they say it is. How convenient. What is good is not something fixed, but whatever they say is good. What is bad today (such as prostitution) may be good tomorrow. Stay tuned. What is beautiful is also determined solely by them. For example, a woman's 'right to choose' is a beautiful thing, even if it ends in the ugly death of her child. But we should not be upset, we are told. The newborn infant will be kept comfortable until the mother and her doctor decide whether it should be put to death, and if so, that will be done in a humane way. Seriously? *Cruel compassion.*

In hell, demons give each other high fives.

If this outrages you, your *uncommon sense* is working!

Wake up, Americans! You have been duped by pretended patriots. Open your eyes! Invisible chains are being forged around your hands and feet. *Is that the future you want?!*

If America is to be one nation *under God*, then we the people must choose to be *under God* and fear God. If we would rather *be* God, then our freedom is justly jeopardized.

Wise up, Americans! Atheistic socialism is the wrong vision. It will lure you down the wrong path with empty promises, bring you decreased wealth with increased misery, and leave you defenseless before those who demean you and wish you ill. If we vote for atheists and socialists, being swayed by their spin and smear and seductive promises, we are betraying the brave Americans who gave us the land of the free!

You must understand more than the media and even our elected officials. With *uncommon sense*, you must grasp America's identity and destiny *under God*.

The atheistic ethical system, with its ferocious rage against God that proclaims freedom from God and His moral law, leads to the death of freedom. Choosing to come under God and under His moral authority leads to liberty. These results seem paradoxical ... but if you understand these realities, you have *uncommon sense*.

Truth is, *"Happy are the people whose God is the Lord"*[86]—and, miserable are the people whose god is the government. If you say "Amen!" then you have *uncommon sense*.

I've got to ask you some questions:

Do you really value security more than liberty?

---

[86] Psalm 144:15

Do you want the government to empower you to create wealth and to distribute wealth as *you* will ... or do you want the government to take care of you from the cradle to the grave, with a hypocritical atheistic elite overseeing universal poverty for all?

Do you want to perpetuate and strengthen the civil rights movement ... or would you rather expand the sexual revolution until we fully replicate Sodom and tempt the judgment of God?

Do you want America to remain a great sovereign nation, ... or become, instead, part of a globalist socialist one world order, a Satanic surveillance society that secretly spies on, systematically suppresses and ruthlessly eliminates all who do not bow before the cruel god of atheistic political correctness?

Do you want to uphold a culture of life in which every human being, including the unborn, has the God-given right to life ... or do you prefer an antichrist culture of death in which abortion and infanticide are the 'sacred' rights of women?

Do you want America to honor the Bible ... or censor it?

Does the battle cry, *"Give me liberty, or give me death!"* sound like the raving of a deranged right-wing fanatic to you? If so, I have more questions for you.

What possesses you that you meekly consent to be regulated by self-appointed elites who have no regard for the life of the unborn or for the rights of any human being?! Why are you willing to be controlled by arrogant atheists who think they know better than you, for whom truth is whatever they make it to be, who feel completely justified in lying to your face, who think that freedom to sin and freedom from God are the loftiest liberties? Freedom *from* God results in the worst slavery. Obedience *to* God results in the most freedom. Don't you understand that without God, you have no God-given rights? That without God, your rights are no longer absolute? That without God, no human life is sacred?

If you take God out of your personal life, out of public life and out of our schools and universities, you create a vacuum; then into this gaping emptiness will step hardened and habitual liars who scorn the Bible, our *Declaration* and the Constitution and who stand in awe, not of God, but of their own intellect! And *to them* you will trust your future?!

More personally: Do you choose the fear of God? Do you choose to believe in and bow before the living God? Do you want your conscience bound by the moral laws of God, or would you rather have the freedom to be as immoral as you want to be?

Most important of all, what is your choice about *Jesus*? Will Jesus be your Lord and Savior? Will the Lord Jesus Christ, the Giver of abundant and eternal life to anyone, anywhere, anytime, be *your* Lord and *your* God?

If you are an atheist, determined to wreck America's moral and spiritual foundations: you are fighting a losing war against God Most High. God is not dead, and you know it. You can't get away from God. You can turn your back on Him and walk into everlasting darkness, or, you can regain your faith in God, your love for liberty and your love for Truth. The choice is yours.

Come to Jesus today!

Jesus made all people to be free.
Atheistic-socialism shackles the soul.

Jesus is the Truth and liberty is His gift. To love lies is to choose chains.

Jesus is Love and He loves us—each of us, personally, passionately, perpetually. Jesus is the Fountain of the sweet love that our world desperately needs.

Jesus is Life and He gives us life as He has it: purposeful life, everlasting life, abundant life.

Jesus is Wisdom and intelligence is His gift. Intelligent people can tell the difference between liberty and anarchy; between prayerful protesting and violent rioting; between constitutional government and autocracy.

Jesus is Holy and virtue is His gift. A people who prefer to be enslaved by sin will be willing to be enslaved by government: they will surrender their rights and liberties to any elected or unelected usurper.

To surrender liberty to gain security is to lose both. To sacrifice privacy to gain safety is to lose both. To swap the living God for freedom to sin is to gain totalitarian government.

A people that forsake their faith will forsake their virtue.

A people that gives up their virtue will give up their freedom.

He who fears God fears nothing else; but a people who do not fear God will fear everything else.

A people who refuse to be ruled by God will be ruled by tyrants.

America is no more destined to be a *secular* nation than a *slave* nation.

The ultimate reality behind our visible universe is a Heart beating with infinite love for everyone; that Heart is revealed in the face of Jesus Christ.

Love is not a molecule; love is a miracle. Love is not an emotion. Love is God in motion.

He who sticks head in bucket should not argue that sun is not shining. He who is infatuated with his own intellect imprisons himself in idiocy. Combining ignorance with arrogance causes calamitous consequence. If your thesis is a lie and your antithesis another lie, your synthesis can only be a really monstrous lie.

He who will not lose his pride will lose every blessing.

He who is not motivated by love will be manipulated by fear.

He who substitutes self for God substitutes light bulb for sun.

He who divorces Jesus to marry the god of self, will wind up in the congregation of the twice dead.

He who represents himself before Judge of universe has fool for client.

If your god isn't working for you, *switch gods*.

Jesus is not into trends. He is into truth. Jesus is the Truth!

Jesus is not a crutch on whom I wobble. Jesus is my Healer who makes me whole so that I run with His fire!

Real freedom, only One can provide: JESUS.

Jesus' freedom is the foundation of *American* freedom.

Jesus is Lord.
Jesus is *my* Lord.
Is He *your* Lord?

AMERICA WILL BE SAVED
by freedom-lovers and freedom-fighters
who personally know the Freedom-Giver,
JESUS CHRIST.
May *you* be one!

May Jesus be your Lord: not just Lord of your heart, but Lord over the totality of your life! *That way, you will not only gain eternal life, but you will be able to join the winning side that triumphantly proclaims:*

America will be saved!

13

WHAT MUST I DO
TO BE SAVED?

**Jesus said: "Go ye into all the world,
and preach the Gospel to every creature.
He that believes and is baptized shall be saved:
but he that believes not shall be damned."[87]**

In the spring of 1776, Tom Paine wrote an essay entitled, *Common Sense*. This essay resonated with Americans because it was pro-Scripture, pro-God and pro-freedom. Paine wrote: *"But where says some is the King of America? I'll tell you, friend, He reigns above."* I like that! Americans back then liked it, and a few months later, adopted the *Declaration of Independence*.

So now, out of love for your immortal soul, I must get personal with you. *Does the King who reigns above reign in your heart? Who exactly is your King? Are you under God? Is Jesus your Lord? You are going to die ... the big question is:*

WHERE WILL YOU SPEND ETERNITY?

---

[87] Mark 16:15-16

I testify: Jesus is my Lord: I am a Christian. Not because the universe God made is so big ... but because God's heart is so big. God loves me in spite of my sin. That gets to me. Jesus saves me from sin. Those who know me, know that I am not a perfect man; they know I need a Savior. I know that more than they do! I'm no better than anyone else. I will tell you what I *know*—not some religious theory.

First, we all need a Savior, because we all have sinned. No one can save himself by his own good works, because the Sovereign God has decreed that only one thing cancels sin: sinless blood. The reality is, you and I have no sinless blood to offer. That is why we cannot save ourselves. *Second,* the free gift of God is eternal life through Jesus Christ. Jesus Christ did have sinless blood: He never sinned. He offered Himself on the cross as the Ultimate Sacrifice for our sin. His resurrection proves that His blood was sinless: that His blood is enough to save us. *Third*, we must take Jesus as our own, and we do that by calling on His Name, and when we do, we receive eternal life!

Someday—perhaps very soon—*you will die.* You will face God. You will stand before the Judgment of Almighty God.

Let's go over the Truth again so you can't claim you didn't know.

You need a Savior. There is only one Savior: Jesus. You either take Him or reject Him. The time for argument is over.

God loves *you*, personally. God's love is not limited to a favored few. God loves everyone. He loves *you*.

Jesus said:

"For God so loved the world (that includes YOU)**, that He gave His only begotten Son, that whosoever** (that's YOU, again!) **believes in Him should not perish, but have everlasting life.**"[88]

---

[88] John 3:16

God wants *you* to have everlasting life: life as He has it. He does not want you to die in your sin and go to a devil's hell. Isn't that wonderful?

I *know* this: *Sin makes us common. Jesus makes us uncommon.* Sin separates us from God who is Love. Jesus connects us to God. Sin kills. Jesus gives life: *abundant* life. I *know* this: *Jesus is the Plus-Maker.* The message of Jesus' death on the cross is moronic nonsense to the hell-bound who refuse to repent of their sin; but to me, it is the life-giving, life-changing power of God!

The cross has two beams: a horizontal beam and a vertical beam. In mathematics, the horizontal beam is a minus sign, and the vertical beam cutting through it is a plus sign.

This is Carl, on his own:

———————————

A big minus. The horizontal beam of Jesus' cross depicts me on my own: one long minus.

Minus speaks of my agony, addictions, my brokenness, my bitterness, my confusion, my depression, my excuses, my fears, my failures, my guilt and my hurts.

Minus speaks of my inability, my loneliness, my misery, my never-ending needs, my problems and my pride.

Minus speaks of my sin, my shame, my sickness, my traumas and my vices.

Minus! What a self-portrait!

Minus is a picture of me on my own—dead in sin, without God. I don't like the way I look without God. My great contribution to the Cross of Jesus is the horizontal beam, the *minus*. That humbles me. I could never, in a million years, turn my *minus* into a *plus*. It gets worse.

You see, *minus* is the will of the devil. You have an unseen enemy who wants you to live and die in *minus*. The devil wants to reduce your entire life to an interminable *miserable MINUS*. The devil wants your eternity to be an *everlasting minus*.

You need to understand *how* this implacable, ruthless enemy works to bring about *minus*. The devil works with two things: *sin*, and *lies*. Sin always brings *minus*. Lies always bring *minus*. As long as you sin, you stay in *minus*. As long as you believe the devil's lies: you stay in *minus*.

But today: the devil won't get his way! Because Jesus came from heaven to earth so He could turn your minus into a plus.

There is Someone who can turn your minus into a plus: *His Name is JESUS!*

Jesus died on purpose, on a cross, to turn our minus into plus.

Jesus chose to die for us! He loves us that much!

You and I could not change our *minus* into *plus*. Never. Not with psychology, not with anything.

Only God Himself could introduce the vertical beam.

THE CROSS IS GOD'S PLUS SIGN.

The Cross is God's way of turning our minus into a plus. PLUS is the will of God for you.

JESUS IS THE PLUS-MAKER.

God saw me mired in my *minus*—and in love to me supplied the vertical beam. I want to shout, "Glory to God!"

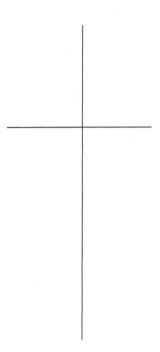

Through His death on the cross, Jesus turns the *minus* of my sin into the *plus* of His salvation!

Jesus alone turns all my minus into plus!!! That's why I sing, *"Can't nobody do me like Jesus!"* That's why Jesus alone is the Savior, why I take Him as *mine*.

You may think you don't need a Savior ... but you do. You may think your good works will save you ... but they won't. There is no such thing as self-salvation! Jesus knew you could not save yourself. If you could have, He would not have died for you. Jesus died on purpose, so that He could turn *your* minus into an everlasting plus. He does not love me anymore than He loves you. Jesus wants PLUS for Y-O-U.

FROM MINUS TO PLUS

A   Jesus turns the minus of my *agonizing addictions*
into the plus of *His affirming acceptance.*

B   Jesus turns the minus of my *brokenness*
into the plus of *His blessing.*

C   Jesus turns the minus of my *curse* and *confusion*
into the plus of *His covenant.*

D   Jesus turns the minus of my *despair* and *dysfunction*
into the plus of *His devil-defeating deliverance.*

E   Jesus turns the minus of my *emptiness*
into the plus of *His energizing enterprise.*

F   Jesus turns the minus of my *failures* and *follies*
into the plus of *His forgiveness.*

F   Jesus turns the minus of my *fears*
into the plus of *His faith.*

G   Jesus turns the minus of my *grief*
into the plus of *His genuine gladness.*

H   Jesus turns the minus of my *hurts and hopelessness*
into the plus of *His healing.*

I   Jesus turns the minus of my *ignorance*
into the plus of *His inspiration* and *illumination.*

L   Jesus turns the minus of my *loneliness*
into the plus of *His limitless love.*

M   Jesus turns the minus of my *misery*
into the plus of *His mighty miracles.*

N   Jesus turns the minus of my *nagging needs*
into the plus of *His never-ending supply.*

O   Jesus turns the minus of my *oppression*
into the plus of *His opportunity.*

P   Jesus turns the minus of my *pain*
into the plus of *His peace.*

Q   Jesus turns the minus of my *quitting*
into the plus of *His quickening.*

R   Jesus turns the minus of my *ruined rancid rags*
into the plus of *His regal robe of righteousness.*

S   Jesus turns the minus of my *slavery to sin*
into the plus of *His sweet salvation.*

T   Jesus turns the minus of my *tragedies*
into the plus of *His triumph.*

U   Jesus turns the minus of my *unbelief*
into the plus of *His unquenchable fire.*

V   Jesus turns the minus of my *vices*
into the plus of *His virtues.*

W   Jesus turns the minus of my *wretchedness*
into the plus of *His warm welcome.*

Y   Jesus turns the minus of my *yielding to sin*
into the plus of a *YES to God.*

Z   Jesus turns the minus of my *zeal for religion*
into the plus a *ZEAL for God and for people!*

When Jesus hung on the Cross, He was fighting for us, to turn all our minus into plus. Love is a warrior. Love fights for what it values, and Jesus values us. Did He lose? What happened on the third day?! He rose from the dead! *Jesus' death proves He is the Ultimate Warrior. Jesus' resurrection proves He is the Ultimate Champion.* This is not lifeless man-made theory: this is Gospel power!

WITHOUT JESUS' DEATH

Without Jesus' death
We are locked in spiritual death
Doomed to be damned,
To be devoured by demons' breath.

Without Jesus' death
For heaven, we are ineligible
Our guilt is never removed, and
Our stains remain indelible.

Without Jesus' death
The curse of sin stays unbroken
The devil's reign of terror uninterrupted
All humanity stays heartbroken.

Without Jesus' death
The love of God cannot reach us
The mercy of God cannot reclaim us
The grace of God cannot lift us.

Without Jesus' death
We cannot be born again from above
Or ever be reconciled to God
Or ever receive His phenomenal love.

Without Jesus' death
Heaven has no door: only hell is open
And we remain eternally poor.
BUT JESUS DIED FOR US!
HE IS THE LIVING DOOR TO HEAVEN!
A DOOR WIDE-OPEN TO ALL,
WHO WANT THEIR SINS FORGIVEN!

THE CROSS OF CHRIST

The Cross of Christ
is God's logo of love
proof undeniable
that He is not detached above.

On the Cross,
Jesus bore our sickness, sin and shame
so that He could give His risen life
to all who call on His Name.

At first the devil gloated,
thinking he had won.
But Christ's Resurrection proved
his evil plans would be undone.

The devil suffered a severe miscalculation.
In heaven there was a mighty celebration:
Satan, the cruel god of this world, now dethroned:
No longer could he claim humanity for his own.
The Champion from heaven had conquered by dying!
Now against the lies of hell there would be a great uprising!

Billions from the guilt and power of sin set free
Enjoying the Jesus Life abundantly
These blood-washed billions, now living unselfishly,
Loving as God loves, passionately;
Changing the world, one life at a time,
What a glorious reality, so sublime!

So, dear friend, receive this Savior right now
Call Him your Lord, and before Him bow!

My friend: We are rewarded for our good works, but we are not saved by them. There are levels of reward in heaven, and I want you to go to heaven, and get a high level of reward! No, we cannot earn or merit our salvation: it is a free gift. We are saved, not by our good works, but by God's.

Friend, hear me. There is a hell after this life. There's no partying in hell. The suffering is too immense. The agony is too intense.

Hell is no joke. Hell is not just hell on earth.

Jesus does not want you to go to hell. *The good news is not that there is a hell: the good news is that you do not have to go!* Jesus Christ bore your sin so you could make heaven and miss hell. No one has to go to hell. But some will.

If you go to hell, it will be your choice, not His. Friend, fear God! He who mocks God's saving grace will suffer God's fiery judgment. He who delights in lying philosophies and specious speculations despises his own mercies. He who stubbornly resists the truth gains a mind utterly void of *uncommon sense*—a reprobate mind—a mind that thinks hell is merely a metaphor.

Hear me! There is no sunshine in hell: only blackness of darkness forever. There is no dawn in hell: only endless night. There is no joy in hell: only unending remorse. There is no love in hell: only hatred. There is no truth in hell: only lies muttered by demons in chains. *I warn you!* Hell is a literal place of eternal burning torment. There is no water there, no cool breezes and no relief from torment. Worst of all, there is no altar call in hell: no grace, no mercy and no more opportunity to repent, to be born again from above.

Oh! My friend! If, somehow, I have not yet persuaded you to shun socialism *AT LEAST DO NOT GIVE THE DEVIL THE SADISTIC SATISFACTION OF SINKING YOUR SOUL INTO HELL! Repent and be saved! End your war against God right now!! Do not delay another second!!!*

Let me lead you in prayer today to be joined to Jesus:

LORD JESUS, I take you right now as my Lord and my Savior.

I believe You died for my sin.

I believe God raised You from the dead: indisputable proof that You are the Son of God, and that Your blood has enough power to blot out all my sin.

I repent of my sin.

LORD JESUS, I CALL ON YOU!

I believe in You!

I belong to You!

By Your grace, in Your strength, I will work with You—to bring Your saving love to others.

Lord Jesus, thank You for saving me, forgiving me all my sin, and making me brand new!

Let everyone know: I AM SAVED! Amen!

Friend, if you prayed that simple prayer with me and meant it, you are now saved. You are now part of the family of God. All your sins are now blotted out, and God remembers them no more. Because you have Jesus, you have life: His resurrection life. You are no longer a hell-bound sinner. You are now a new creature in Christ Jesus, a blood-washed child of the living God. *Amen!*

Begin to read the Bible, and let the Word of God revamp your morality. Read the Bible with the intent to put into practice what you read. Learn to think God's thoughts after Him so you can imitate Him. You have been conformed to a culture created by atheists and hedonists; now you must be transformed into the moral image of Jesus. How is such total transformation possible? *God's Word is the most powerful change agent in the universe.*

Your heart has been changed—now your mind must catch up. The way you think determines the way you live. God's Word will transform the way you think.

Join a good local church, whose Pastor is committed to making you a disciple of your Lord Jesus Christ.

Your faith and your morality are personal, but they must both find public expression. You are now the salt of the earth and the light of the world. There is a power inside you that must be developed and unleashed—that will lift America to new heights of freedom and justice.

Jesus not only turns our minus into plus, He turns *us* into plus. Without Jesus, you and I were a minus—subtracting good from every situation. Now, because of what Jesus has done, we are a plus—we add value to every situation. We add life and love and blessing. We add wisdom and creativity and joy. This is why there is hope for America. *You* are now a plus!

Some see only America's sins and become depressed, as if they were helpless spectators on a sinking ship. I say: *America is not the Titanic. America is not Sodom. America belongs to Jesus!*

Your choices—and your votes—matter. God has given the privilege of charting our nation's future to its citizens, to you and to me. God needs your voice in the earth. He needs you to speak words of faith and hope over your nation. We must not be negative or lazy; we must have bravery and backbone that last longer than one election. We must be committed for *decades*. Of course, we must grasp the dire seriousness of our time; but we must embrace the sure prophecy with unwavering anticipation of its soon fulfillment:

America will be saved!

14

UNCOMMON FAITH

**Jesus said, "All things are possible
to him that believes."**[89]

America will be saved. That is my faith. My heart's desire. My
passion. *Jesus* wants America to be saved. And, if Jesus wants it, then
I want it. The Lord Jesus Christ, by the Holy Spirit, gave the late
Reinhard Bonnke this simple word of prophecy: *"America will be
saved!"*

True prophecies reveal God's will.

But God's will does not come to pass automatically, as we sit on
our sofas doing nothing or as we hide under them in fear! God does
not work in our lives apart from us: He works in us through our faith.
Prophecies are meant to create faith. Heart faith knows the will of
God and refuses to accept what is not God's will. It is not God's will
that America be destroyed. It is God's will that America be saved!

*The purpose of prophecy is to create in us bold, triumphant,
active faith—a faith that sees the invisible and that believes God for
the impossible. We need prophecy to jar us out of unbelief, fear and
mental reasoning.*

---

[89] Mark 9:23

Faith is not assent; faith is action. Faith is acting on the Word of God. Head faith is a theological position. In contrast, heart faith is hope-filled action based on the revealed will of God. Heart faith is *uncommon faith*, faith that will change a nation. Faith not just for my personal needs, but faith for an entire nation ... imagine that!

Uncommon faith is a victorious battle. Unseen enemies—demons—do not want God's will for America to come to pass. These very real enemies are vicious, ruthless and dead set on America's destruction. They hope that we believers will stay passive or ignorant or carnal or petrified. Let us destroy their foul hopes, in Jesus' Name!

Desperation, outrage and horror are not uncommon faith, but they can be fuel for it and for perseverance.

THE EYE OF FAITH

If all we see is what we see, then we will never change what we see.

God gives us, first, His written Word, and second, a prophetic word, to give us something unseen to see. Uncommon faith holds fast to a God-supplied vision.

Uncommon faith sees unseen realities; and then, being so thrilled with these as yet invisible realities, dares to declare what God has declared, in the face of contradictory evidence, knowing that the invisible will become visible.

Uncommon faith comes by hearing the Word of God and is released by our words. Our words of faith are a response to His Word and harmonize with His Word.

Uncommon faith is a rational choice. It is perfectly rational to trust the God who cannot lie.

When we see the unseen with the eye of faith, then what we see with our physical eyes ceases to matter. God's revelation of unseen reality is meant to transform what we see and say—and ultimately what we have. When faced with any negative, we need a greater positive. Not a positive born out of the human mind—but a positive born of God.

God sees from a different perspective than we do. In order to work with God, we have to see as He sees. First, we have to see ourselves as God sees us. We have to see our identity and our inheritance in Christ Jesus, otherwise, we will live as mere unchanged, unsaved people. We are saints, not scum. We are believers, not beggars. We are new creatures, not nameless nobodies. We are victors, not victims. We are God's workmanship, not junk. We are more than conquerors. We are part of the Church: called out of mundane living to be part of a privileged group that by prayer and the obedience of faith determines national affairs for the benefit of all. We have the faith of God, the love of God, the grace of God, the armor of God, including the most powerful weapon on the planet: the spoken Word of God; we have the authority of Jesus, the Blood of Jesus and the Name of Jesus. All this, in addition to our right to vote.

God works in us and through us according to what we believe and say. Jesus revealed these realities when He said, *"Out of the abundance of the heart the mouth speaks"* and again, *"Whosoever shall have whatsoever he says."*[90]

So, when God inspires a brother or sister in the Lord to prophesy, He has an end in mind and He is working toward that end. He knows that He is limited by what we believe and speak. He knows that if we believe only what we see, and speak only what we have, then what He wants will not come to pass. When God gives a prophecy, He intends to change what we see. He is working from the inside to the outside.

133

---

[90] Matthew 12:34; Mark 11:23

What does God want to come to pass? He wants America to be saved. There is enough power in the four words, *America will be saved,* to make it reality in our lifetime. God believes and expects that we will respond in faith to what He has said, knowing that our faith will unleash His almighty power.

Remember the Bible account when the Spirit of God carried the prophet Ezekiel into a valley full of bones? There the bones lay exposed: dead, dry, disconnected. *That valley is a picture of America.* God asked the prophet if the bones could live. He sidestepped and replied, *"O LORD God, You know."*[91] He didn't know, but he knew that God knew. And God specializes in raising the dead to life! Twice, Ezekiel was commanded to prophesy:

> "Prophesy upon these bones, and say unto them, O ye dry bones, hear the word of the Lord ... *So I prophesied as I was commanded:* and as I prophesied, there was noise, and behold a shaking, and the bones came together, bone to his bone. And when I beheld, lo, the sinews and the flesh came up upon them, and the skin covered them above: but here was no breath in them. Then He said unto me, Prophesy unto the wind, prophesy, son of man, and say to the wind, Thus saith the LORD God; Come from the four winds, O breath, and breathe upon these slain, that they may live. *So I prophesied as He commanded me,* and the breath came into them, and they lived, and stood up upon their feet, an exceeding great army."[92]

God wanted those bones to come together and come alive, but He could not make it happen without Ezekiel's intelligent and trusting participation. God wants America to be saved, but He can't do it with your mouth shut, or with you speaking unbelief, or with you lazily leaving the Great Commission to others.

---

[91] Ezekiel 37:3
[92] Read Ezekiel 37:1-14

"God is in control" is religious sentiment inducing laziness.

"God answers prayer" is true hope inspiring intercession.

God works when we work, is Bible Truth.

We have three parties: God, the devil, and you, each releasing something. God has released power to bring heaven on earth. The devil releases hell on earth. You are to release faith, hope and love! God's power is dormant until someone releases uncommon faith. Uncommon faith thwarts the devil by activating God's power. Your faith in the prophetic word that God gives brings the power of God into your nation! A prophecy presents a picture of what can be and should be, and what will be, if we respond in lion-like faith. True prophecy is not man's opinion or a product of man's imagination, but is a message direct from God Himself through a sanctified human vessel. You have to answer this question: "Is God behind the prophecy, *"America will be saved"?* Is He, or isn't He? If He isn't, then America is going down, and there's no stopping its pathetic demise. I press the issue: Did Brother Bonnke prophesy as he was commanded? If the answer is YES! then America *can* be saved, no matter what it looks like. But you must add your faith!

*"And it shall come to pass in the last days, saith God, I will pour out of My Spirit upon all flesh: and **your sons and your daughters shall prophesy** ... on My servants and on My handmaidens I will pour out in those days of My Spirit; and **they shall prophesy.**"*[93]

*"Quench not the Spirit. **Despise not prophesyings**; prove all things: hold fast that which is good."*[94]

*"This charge I commit unto thee, son Timothy, according to **the prophecies** which went before on thee, **that thou by them** mightiest war a good warfare."*[95]

135

[93] Acts 2:17-18
[94] 1 Thessalonians 5:19-21
[95] 1 Timothy 1:18

The Holy Spirit inspired the Scriptures, the alone authoritative standard by which every opinion, interpretation, sermon, commentary or prophecy is measured.

Today the same Spirit moves upon men and women of God to teach and preach in line with Scripture, and also flames in their soul to prophecy *so that we by their inspired prophecies might fight the good fight of faith.*

How does prophecy differ from preaching? Both proclaim Truth, but prophecy comes from the unexpected inspiration of the Holy Spirit, while preaching comes from diligent study of Scripture. The preacher expertly explains Scripture. But the one who prophecies speaks from the sudden and spontaneous moving of the Holy Spirit.

God in His majestic sovereignty has given you and me free will, and He prefers that we use it to bring heaven to earth. If we misuse our free will, we bring hell to earth. If, instead of believing the Word of the God who cannot lie, we believe lies and speak according to what we feel, we will miss our destiny and the prophecy that should have and could have come to pass ... will lie unfulfilled.

The choice is ours. God cannot control what we choose. We are not puppets; He is not the puppet Master. Believing is a choice. Believing is an act of the will. Bible faith is believing in line with the Bible.

The world might say, "Believe!" but the key issue is: What do we believe? Whom do we believe? Why do we believe?

My answer: *In God I trust!* Why? It is impossible for God to lie!

What is your answer? In whom do you trust?

To trust God is to trust His Word, including His prophetic word. It is absurd to assert, "I believe God, but I don't believe what He says."

Blind faith is not Bible faith. Real faith is not "a leap into the dark." Real faith is a step into the light—into the light of God's Word. God's Word gives light.

God said, through His dedicated servant, now in heaven, *"America will be saved!"*

TWO RESPONSES

When God speaks through His servants, people respond in two ways: they either believe or scoff. Both responses are a decision. Your response is up to you.

Before you make your final decision about whether the prophesy *"America will be saved!"* is truth or fiction, allow me to remind you of two Bible stories that depict these two responses of believing or scoffing, and the dramatically different outcomes produced.

The first case is the positive response of believing inspired prophecy. The nation of Judah, the southern kingdom of Israel, was under attack—not by one enemy, but by three.[96]

You might ask, "Why were they in such a terrible dilemma?" The answer: their leadership had betrayed them.

Here is a significant lesson: *No nation can rise above its spiritual leadership.*

The king of Judah had *"joined affinity with Ahab"*—he had helped the man who hated God. Therefore, wrath was upon him from the Lord, and His wrath meant that He would no longer protect them from those who wanted them dead. And so, the enemies of Judah came out to destroy them. The king finally came to his senses and humbled himself. Yes, he fasted and prayed. He was so desperate for God's help that he stopped eating and prayed in earnest.

96 Please read 2 Chronicles 18-20

God is so good. God is so merciful. When we repent, He gives us mercy: not because we deserve it, but because He is good. God delights in a broken and contrite heart.

As the king and all the people bowed in God's presence, waiting for His answer, the Spirit of the Lord came upon a man from the priestly tribe of Levi, and he prophesied:

"Thus saith the LORD unto you, Be not afraid nor dismayed by reason of this great multitude: for the battle is not yours, but God's ... Ye shall not need to fight in this battle ... fear not, nor be dismayed; tomorrow go out against them: for the LORD will be with you."

The King, Jehoshaphat, was so grateful for this strong prophetic word; he simply believed the prophecy and began to worship the Lord and then he led the Levites in praising the Lord God with a loud voice. The next morning, Jehoshaphat made a tremendously important declaration:

"Believe in the Lord your God, so shall ye be established; believe His prophets, so shall ye prosper."

All the people chose to believe what had been prophesied. The result was supernatural: their enemies fought each other. Instead of launching an attack against Judah, their enemies annihilated each other. The people of Judah just watched in amazement, and it took them three days to gather up the spoils of war—a war in which they did not fight. What was their part? They believed the prophet of God, and they praised God in advance of victory as if victory was already won.

What is the pertinent principle?

Believing the Word of God gives you the ability to stand strong; believing the prophecies of the prophets of the Lord will cause you to succeed supernaturally.

Perhaps it is providential that the reference for this verse is 2 Chronicles 20:20. Think about 20/20 vision, about the year 2020, about the decade of the 2020s. The 1920s were known as the roaring twenties—when the flesh roared.

The 2020s will be known as the decade when the Lion of Judah, the Spirit of God and the people of God roared in unison: ***AMERICA WILL BE SAVED!***

Let me give you the other example, the negative response of scoffing at an inspired prophetic word.[97]

Wicked Ahab had died and his son had become king, and continued the wickedness of his father, rebelling against the moral law of God. Because of their unrestrained depravity, disaster befell the northern kingdom of Israel: the Syrians came and besieged the capitol, Samaria, and reduced it to starvation. Inside the city was a true prophet of God, Elisha. Both the king of Syria and the king of Israel wanted him dead! The very day that the king of Israel made up his mind to assassinate Elisha, God stepped in. Elisha prophesied. He said, *"Hear ye the word of the LORD; Thus saith the LORD, Tomorrow about this time*—now I will paraphrase—*the famine will be over and you will enjoy abundance!"* What a prophecy! An unnamed confidant of the king scoffed. With mocking derision, he dismissed the prophet: *"Behold, if the Lord would make windows in heaven, might this thing be?"* In other words, "You are a lunatic and your prophecy is lunacy. Even your God couldn't make it come true!" God heard it, and God is not mocked.

---

[97] Please read 2 Kings 6:8-33, chapter 7, Elisha did not know how his prophecy would be fulfilled. It was fulfilled, in a most unlikely way. God's business is to figure out the "how." Our business is to trust Him and obey His specific leading. **Seek God for what He wants YOU to do!**

The prophet prophesied again: *"Behold, you shall see it with your eyes, but you shall not eat one bite of the abundance."* What happened? This prophecy also came to pass. The abundance came, and the people rushed on it in their hunger, and the mocking confidant was run over, trampled to death, seeing the miracle but not tasting one bite. He heard both prophecies, but chose to scoff.

Here is a great lesson: Mockers miss sweet salvation. Here is another: Choices have consequences attached. God has done the attaching: that is part of His sovereign privilege as God. We do the choosing: that is part of our privilege as people made in God's image.

You can choose to believe the lying promises of lying politicians—and you can choose to believe the lying accusations and the lying analysis of mocking media—if that's what you want to do. But there are consequences attached. If you scoff at the prophecy, *America will be saved*—you will be left out when God sweeps in.

As for me and my house, we choose to believe the Lord. We choose to believe His prophets. We choose to believe the prophecy: *America will be saved!* I'm a believer. I'm not naïve or gullible.

I walk by faith, because I know these three things: (1) *What God says is, is*—though it is unseen; (2) *What is, has the potential to change what is seen; (3) Faith speaks of what is, as though it already were, and that is what causes it to be seen.* This is why I need *you* to join me in faith!

SAVED *FROM* ... SAVED *FOR* ... SAVED *HOW?*

America will be saved! Saved *from* what? Saved from sin, the devil and doctrines of devils! Saved from perversion, debauchery and narcissistic hedonism! Saved from hatred, racism and racial division! Saved from a drug epidemic, violence and anarchy! Saved from plagues, pestilences and pandemics! Saved from corruption, tyranny and atheistic socialism! Saved from the seductive rhetoric of Marxism! Saved from those who would overthrow our Constitution!

The children of Israel were saved from slavery in Egypt; they were delivered out of cruel bondage, out of brutal and merciless oppression. But that was only *half* the plan. God brought them *out* so He could bring them *in*. He always intended to fulfill His promise to Abraham, Isaac and Jacob, that His chosen people would possess the land of milk and honey, the land of Canaan, the Promised Land.

America will be saved.

Saved *for* what? Saved for the purposes of God, that we may fulfill our national destiny under God to advance the Christian faith!

Saved *how*? Saved by the fiery preaching of the Gospel! Saved by a mighty outpouring of God's Holy Spirit as we preach!

Nothing less than a Great Awakening will keep America from being slain by the demon of atheistic socialism. Only one thing can save America: The Gospel! But for the Gospel to do its saving work, it must be preached by us in the power of the Holy Spirit. A non-supernatural Gospel is no Gospel. The real Gospel is supernatural, miraculous and nation-saving.

Passionate preaching produces Great Awakening.

This is where *you* come in! A Christian who does not preach is like a light that does not shine. You do not need a church pulpit to preach. Your "pulpit" may be social media.

GREAT AWAKENING!

What is Great Awakening?

Great Awakening is when JESUS takes center stage, when all eyes are on JESUS, and when multiplied millions are drawn to Him! It is called *Great* because it overwhelms, overcomes and overpowers the dark onslaught of secularism, atheism, Marxism, socialism, Communism and hedonism. It is called an *Awakening* because prior to, the people were in a drunken stupor, sadly unaware of their devil's wicked plans for their destruction.

A Great Awakening is more than an emotional high: it is a cultural reset.

A *Great Awakening is Revival and Reformation.*

A Church in *Revival* is on fire: it is feasting on the meat of God's Word; it is passionately praying, walking in holiness, demonstrating the love of God to all, manifesting all the gifts of the Holy Spirit, and going into all the world to seek and to save the lost. *Reformation* means that the morals and the laws of society are changed to harmonize with the moral character and moral law of Almighty God.

A Great Awakening is the Church at its full potential: full of grace and glory, full of faith and life, full of love and power.

Great Awakening begins with a radical reprioritizing of our lives, a fundamental reordering of our desires. Great Awakening is a stunning inversion, so that what used to be first and foremost: sports, entertainment, education, clothes and making money, we de-idolize; and what used to be non-essential interruption: Bible reading, prayer, church attending, good works and winning souls, we make first and foremost.

Great Awakening is nationwide awakening to the sobering reality that our ways have displeased God. Great Awakening is nationwide awakening to the sublime reality that holiness is the fountain of happiness. Great Awakening is nationwide awakening to the surprising reality that the grace of God is His ability at work in us. Great Awakening is nationwide awakening to the startling reality of Jesus' literal, soon return. Great Awakening is intelligent recognition of who the living God is, coupled with passionate devotion to Him and wholehearted obedience to His moral law of love. Great Awakening is exchanging the love of sin for the love of righteousness. Great Awakening is embracing a culture of life and eradicating a culture of death. Great Awakening is the fire of God blazing in our hearts, burning up every trace of sin, burning in to us the moral image of Jesus, and fueling our joyful obedience to the will of God.

In 2001, when Islamic terrorists attacked America, it was an opportunity for Americans to wake up. Most kept sleeping, oblivious to the antichrist powers at work behind the scenes. In late 2020, as I write this, the damnable COVID-19 pandemic is another wake-up call. Will we press the snooze button again? Will we be content just to return to "normal" or worse, a "new normal" orchestrated by those who hate God and who want to mask and muzzle the Church?

If you can read, the handwriting is on the wall: antichrist spirits want America to fall into the hands of tyrants who have no fear of God!

Let us wake up right now, in Jesus' Name! Let GREAT AWAKENING SWEEP OUR NATION! Great Awakening is birthed out of the hunger and thirst of believers ... the great question is: *how hungry are you? ... how thirsty are you?*

Friend, I want the fire of God to blaze hot *in you,* so that you come to God, walk with God and live a life on fire for God. *You* can be and must be a catalyst for Great Awakening. God needs *you. You are vital, because God's plan includes you.* No matter what it looks like, I have unshakable assurance in my heart that God-given prophecy will be fulfilled: ***AMERICA WILL BE SAVED! YOU*** are a catalyst to make it happen. God wants to use you as a supernatural catalyst to ignite Great Awakening in America that will spread swiftly to the entire world. That is your divine destiny.

YOU: A CATALYST

A catalyst is inherently different than other substances. In science, a catalyst speeds up a chemical reaction and lowers the amount of energy needed to make that reaction happen. An enzyme is an example of a catalyst; think of a digestive enzyme that speeds up the digestion of beans and makes it easier for your body to digest such foods. In a broader, non-scientific sense, a catalyst is a stimulating force that causes change. A catalyst gets things going.

Let's apply that to you. Jesus has made you different so you can make a difference. Because the Holy Spirit lives in you, you are designed to get things going that are at a stand-still. Something in your inner man has the capacity to cause cultural change. That something is the holy anointing of God—the same anointing that raised Jesus from the dead.

Now here is a sobering thought. In science, a catalyst can be degraded—that is, its chemical make-up can be changed, and then it no longer is a catalyst.

Let's apply that to you. It is easy to be entertained by our immoral entertainment industry; it is easy to listen to the atheistic media and become a petrified do-nothing believer mired in pessimism and passivity. It is easy to lose cool off, lose the blazing fire of God and the holy urgency that *now* is the time to bring Awakening to America. It is much easier to analyze America's ailments and much more comfortable to do nothing; it requires less consecration (really, none at all) to be a critic or a spectator or an analyst.

There's only one problem: you're not called to be an *analyst:* you're called to be a *catalyst*.

The great question is: What does it take to be a catalyst for Jesus? The answer: You must be ALL IN.

ARE YOU ALL-IN?

What does it mean to be ALL IN? Think of these contrasts.

A convert is in. A disciple is ALL IN. A convert is *in Christ*. A disciple is a partner with Jesus in the great work of plundering hell and populating heaven. A convert is content just going to heaven and prefers to stay carnal. A disciple is dissatisfied unless he sees the will of God come to pass: Revival, Reformation and Great Awakening!

ALL IN means that our Lord Jesus Christ is our first love: He reigns in our heart without rival.

ALL IN means that we are fearless in the face of persecution: we are unashamed of Jesus and His Gospel.

ALL IN means we are on fire for Jesus.

ALL IN means we go *all out* for Jesus.

ALL IN means we go *all the way* to expand His Kingdom.

As ALL-IN catalysts for Jesus, we enable the Spirit of God to move on the hearts of people who otherwise would never be reached.

As ALL-IN catalysts for Jesus, we accelerate significant change in the hearts and lives of people. You can't live the 'normal' Christian life and be a catalyst for Jesus.

How do you become, and stay, a catalyst?

Begin with Jesus. Jesus my Lord was ALL IN. He died on the cross for me and for you. You can't get more ALL IN than that. If Jesus was ALL IN yesterday, then He's ALL IN today and He'll be ALL IN forever. Jesus is ALL IN today, for you. Now, respond to Jesus; let the Spirit of God move you to match His "all-in-ness"!

I like people who are ALL IN for Jesus. I look up to anyone who is ALL IN for Jesus.

Richard Wurmbrand (1909-2001) was ALL IN. Richard, Founder of *The Voice of the Martyrs*, after having spent 14 years being imprisoned and tortured by Communists, wrote *Tortured for Christ*, in which he stated: *"Christians are often half-heartedly on the side of the whole truth. Communists are wholeheartedly on the side of the lie."*[98] That boils my blood!

---

[98] Richard Wurmbrand, *Tortured for Christ*, Living Sacrifice Book Company, Bartlesville, OK, 1967, 1998, p. 86.

Isaac Watts (1674-1748) was ALL IN. After reflecting on Jesus' great love for us, Isaac wrote *When I Survey the Wondrous Cross*, which concludes: "*Love so amazing, so divine, demands my soul, my life, my all.*"[99] Jesus gets my soul, my life, my *all*. That's what you say and sing when you're ALL IN for Jesus!

Being ALL IN has nothing to do with your age. Being all in has nothing to do with your personality. Being all in has nothing to do with your skin color, your gender or your level of education. You're not too young and you're never too old to live ALL IN. *You never retire from being ALL IN!* Being ALL IN is a matter of your heart and your character, not a matter of your personality or gifting: *everyone* can be ALL IN.

When you're ALL IN, you will have a sense of urgency: you've got to do something *today* to win lost souls. When you're ALL IN, you will have a spirit of prayer: you'll be quick to pray fervently in the spirit. When you're ALL IN, you won't have to be begged to give to missions: you will refuse to let the devil minimize your life through stinginess or fear. You will give radically—like the woman with alabaster box. Her giving was so extravagant it got Judas upset. Do you have her spirit or his? Are you stealing God's tithes and offerings, or gladly giving more than you can? When you're ALL IN, you don't play with drugs, alcohol, pornography—or any other sin. You don't play: you're in a war. You are contending: *"My generation belongs to Jesus. My nation belongs to Jesus."* You are busy preaching with the fire of God burning in your soul, whether on social media or in person, to one or to ten thousand: *"Jesus saves, heals and delivers!"*

Atheism is built on lies. I don't want to be part of a nation built on lies: I want to be part of a nation build on Truth, on eternal Truth. America was destined to be ONE NATION UNDER GOD—not an atheistic nation without God.

[99] Isaac Watts, *When I Survey the Wondrous Cross*, 1707; verse 4.

Make no mistake, the devil knows the prophecy: *America will be saved*. He is doing his best to make God a liar. It is the devil who unleashes destruction on nations, not God. The devil is a liar-thief-murderer who aims only to steal, kill and destroy. Deception is the work of the devil.

Pestilences and pandemics, and disease and death are not the work of God—but the work of the devil. The only sense in which the "birth pangs" of the end times are the judgment of God is that they are His *passive* or *unwilling* judgment: He lets us reap what we sow. As stated in Romans 1, three times, God abandons the wicked: He gives them over to a reprobate, senseless, worthless mind. God unwillingly allows what is not His will. God's *active* judgment was at Calvary, where on the Cross He laid all our sin on His Son. That was God's *preferred* judgment. The judgment rendered by virtue of what Jesus did in His death, burial and resurrection is that all who believe on Him are no more beggars, but believers, authorized to resist the devil and to bring his evil plans to nothing. It is high time that we walk in the light of this favorable judgment! God wills that we come under His authority so that we can exercise His authority and stop the destruction and devastation brought by devils, often through human hands.

If we, as a nation, foolishly despise God's active judgment at Calvary, then all that is left is to suffer His passive judgments. National wickedness brings national calamity. National repentance will bring national blessing. If we repent and come under God's authority, we will escape the cruel authority of devil-inspired, power-drunk elitists. For America to be spared the passive judgments of God and for America to receive a visitation from God that results in prolonged prosperity and liberty, America must be saved from sin and pride and come back to a place of godliness and heart faith.

Can America really be saved?

The question really is: Is there a Savior who can save us to the uttermost, who loves us too much to let us miss our destiny, who can turn the wreckage of our lives into a living testimony of His miracle power? *Yes, there is.*

Is there a Savior who can forgive us all our sin, make us completely new, and give us a new status as sons and daughters of Almighty God? *Yes, there is.*

Is there a Savior who can remove our heart of stone and replace it with a tender heart of love? *Yes, there is.*

Is there a Savior who can give us His heart, put His Spirit in us, and write His moral law on our minds? *Yes, there is.*

Is there a Savior whose Blood is powerful enough to cleanse our defiled conscience, who can deliver us from the guilt, the addictive power and the awful curse of sin? *Yes, there is.*

Is there a Savior who loved us enough to die for us, who is mighty enough to have risen from the dead, and who can not only raise us out of spiritual death but also impart to us His own risen life? *Yes, there is.*

Is there a Savior who is the same, yesterday and today and forever, who can fill our hearts with His own faith, and who can fill us with the Holy Spirit as on the Day of Pentecost? *Yes, there is.*

Is there a Savior who can give us almighty grace so our lives will be a showcase of His fire, not a spectacle of our flesh? *Yes, there is.*

JESUS is His Name! He is my Savior, and I trust by now He is yours, as well.

Therefore:

America will be saved!

15

My Challenge
to America's
Spiritual Leadership

**But as truly as I live,
all the earth shall be filled
with the glory of the Lord.**[100]

**And it shall come to pass in the last days,
saith God,
I will pour out of My Spirit upon all flesh.**[101]

O Lord God, do as You have said![102]

Jesus saves us, then makes us His *uncommon* partners.

Just as we need Jesus to be saved, Jesus needs *us* for America to be saved.

---

[100] Numbers 14:21
[101] Acts 2:17
[102] 2 Samuel 7:25

The Holy Spirit spoke through Isaiah the prophet:

"Arise!"[103]Arise from your lethargy! Arise from your self-pity! Arise from your apathy! Arise from your passivity! Arise from your depravity! Arise from your debauchery! Arise from the dust of despair! *Arise* is a strong word. *Arise* means, wake up! Get up! You have been mesmerized and misinformed by the media: you've been burning daylight!

"Arise, shine!" Arise with purpose! Arise with passion! Arise to your blood-bought seating next to Jesus! Arise to the unseen reality that you are seated with Him in heavenly places, in a place of authority. Arise and evangelize! God didn't tell you to shelter in place: He told you to go into all the world! Let the bright hope of the Gospel shine through your loving witness!

"Arise, shine; for thy light is come, and the glory of the Lord is risen upon thee." Do NOT judge only according to what you see or hear. Judge according to Scripture. The Lord Jesus has come from heaven, died on a cross, rose from the dead, poured out His Holy Spirit, and brought the light of revelation Truth to you.

"For, behold, the darkness shall cover the earth, and gross darkness the people." The darkness of demonic deception has spread like dense fog and smog over the entire earth. **Political correctness is gross darkness**: darkness so thick the people are literally blinded to Truth and reality. Along with dark deception, fear. Everything that can be shaken, will be shaken.

"But!"

In the midst of this darkness. In the midst of this gross darkness. In the midst of panic and fear, one word: **"But!"** *But* is God's word to interrupt the devil's madness. *But* means: God is not done!

---

[103] Isaiah 60:1-2

God never surrenders to the darkness. The God who said, *"Let there be light!"* has a plan for America! In dark times, His light really shines!

"But the LORD shall arise upon thee, and His glory shall be seen upon thee."

Divine Intervention can save America! That's where *you* come in! *"Arise, shine ... the LORD shall arise."* We arise first; then God arises! He cannot arise on us in power until we arise in faith. We can and must claim the glory of God to be made manifest on us!

Consider this: You and I are part of the people of God. The *Constitution of the United States* begins with the phrase, *"We, the People."* God made a glorious promise to Israel beginning with these three words, *"If My people."*

"IF MY PEOPLE, which are called by My name, shall humble themselves, and pray, and seek My face, and turn from their wicked ways; then will I hear from heaven, and will forgive their sin, and will heal their land."[104]

So, we have "We, the People" and "My people"—a people within a people. We *His* people are supposed to influence "We, *the* People." *The future of America is in the hands of the people of God.* This truth gives me hope and challenges me at the same time. We believers are stewards of our nation! We are not helpless, powerless, defenseless spectators, only able to *watch* the news and wring our hands and submit to the "experts." **We can change the news! By the obedience of faith, we can bring down on our nation the mercy of our God and the saving power of our God!**

---

[104] 2 Chronicles 7:14; v13 speaks of the judgment of pestilence. *Pestilence* is one of God's passive judgments. When a nation is struck with a passive judgment at the hands of the devil, we believers must wake up, pray and use our authority to stop the judgment. God's active judgment was Jesus' death, and we are to live, pray and work in light of that favorable judgment!

God's promise of national revival was first made to the nation of Israel, but it applies to any nation. *Americans can claim it for America!* God's promise is conditional. There are three conditions or requirements that we must fulfill, *before* God can keep His promise. The good news is that God freely gives us sufficient grace so that we can meet the conditions. What are they? (1) *Humility (2) Passionate Prayer (3) Holiness of heart and life.*

#1 – HUMILITY: *We must humble ourselves: we must get down on our knees and fast. We need God! We need His mercy, His grace, His wisdom, His protection and His intervention! When you are hungrier for mercy and a move of God than for donuts, you are hungry enough.*

#2 – PASSIONATE PRAYER: *We must pray and seek God's face. We've got to tune everything out and press into God's holy presence with all the seriousness of our soul.*

#3 – HOLINESS OF HEART AND LIFE: *We must turn from our wicked ways. We must confess our sin and forsake it by the power of grace. We cannot buy into false grace and its lies that we are already forgiven and have no need to repent!*

These three requirements are lifelong responsibilities demanding of us constant vigilance, not just until a particular crisis passes or the political party we prefer comes to power.

Why is *humility* a necessary condition? Because God resists the proud and gives grace to the humble.

Why is *passionate prayer* an essential condition? Because we cannot bind the outpouring of satanic influence or loose a mighty outpouring of the Holy Spirit, without passionate prayer. God is limited by our prayer life: by how we pray in private, with our families, and with our local churches. He only acts in answer to our prayers of faith.

Why is *holiness of heart and life* a wise condition? Because without holiness, we become lukewarm. Because impurity robs us of the fire of God, short-circuits the power of God, blocks the glory of God, and sabotages the anointing of God.

I reiterate: It is the privilege and duty of *"We, HIS People"* to orchestrate the change our nation needs, but we must be in position to do so. By fulfilling those three conditions, we get in position. Rejecting *com*promise qualifies us for the promise. Blaming secular humanists or the devil will not solve our national problems. Since *"We, His People"* are the determining factor in what laws our nation has, then the kind of government our nation has is what we deserve. We believers must take responsibility for the future of our nation. We determine our nation's identity, destiny and future by our humility, prayers and holiness. *God's intervention is limited by our obedience! God can only bless us to the level of our obedience!*

I must return to the issue of *passionate prayer*. Do our prayers have the fire, the focus and the faith to move God?

Think about a man named Caleb. On his 85th birthday, he had one thing burning in his soul; it was his birthday present. *"Give me this mountain!"* he asked Joshua. "Give me this mountain full of giants—the very giants that intimidated all Israel years ago, that delayed my entrance into the Promised Land for 40 years. I don't want a rocking chair on my back porch facing the sunset. I don't want to retire in quiet tranquility. I don't want a lakefront home overlooking the Dead Sea. I'm ready for war! I am as strong this day as I was 45 years ago. GIVE ME THIS MOUNTAIN!"[105] I can almost hear the roar in his voice. And that inspires me! That stirs me!

If Jesus were to stand in front of you and ask you, "What do you want for your birthday this year?" What would you tell Him?

[105] Read the account in Joshua 14:6-14

"Give me souls! Give me this subdivision! Give me this apartment complex! Give me this business! Give me souls! Give me this city! Give me this school! Give me this university!"

Or this:

GIVE ME AMERICA!

Why not?! Why not, ask big? Why not, ask for something beyond what you think is possible?

Perhaps you feel you are too old to go: but you are not too old to pray with passion! You can pray that God will raise up men and women to go! You can pray that God will call, train, anoint, and thrust out into the harvest fields tens of thousands of believers, all with the fire of God burning in their hearts! Your fire, your focus and your faith are essential to what God wants to do in this window of time before Jesus returns. *Your* unshakable commitment to the Lord Jesus Christ is a catalyst for the change God desires today. You are a difference-maker. You are a history-maker. *Your heavenly calling is to be a flame of fire that brings Great Awakening to America!*

William Bradford (1590-1657), who came to America on the Mayflower in 1620, was a zealous Puritan, a sincere Christian and a government leader with great integrity. On his tombstone is this inscription, written in Latin:[106]

**What our fathers
with so much difficulty attained
do not basely relinquish.**

What a fiery challenge! May you hear this challenge when you lie down to sleep and when you wake up in the morning!

Do not surrender America to those who hate God!

154

---

[106] Federer, p. 67.

It reminds me of what Naboth said to Ahab, *"The LORD forbid that I should give the inheritance of my fathers unto you!"*[107] Naboth stood up against the king and his demon-possessed wife. His vineyard was his inheritance, and "for the sake of peace" he could not give it to Ahab and Jezebel. What will you do with your vineyard? *America is your inheritance.* Surely, you will not relinquish it to those who despise God!

What is Jesus saying to us today? What is His "now" word?

"Occupy till I come!"[108]

Jesus is coming—and until then, He expects us to be busy doing the Father's salvation business. *Occupying* means preaching the Gospel. *Occupying* means building up the local church. *Occupying* means winning souls to Jesus. *Occupying* means doing all the good we can to others. *Occupying means bringing our nation and all nations to the obedience of faith!* Jesus said for us to occupy until He came, knowing full well that the time period immediately before His coming would be marked by increased opposition and difficulty, famines, pestilences, earthquakes, wars, iniquity abounding, deception, hatred and betrayal. *None of that cancels our commission. None of that annuls our assignment.* In the parable of the pounds (Luke 19:11-27), the pound is the Gospel. Jesus is telling us to use this sacred God-given treasure to the utmost to win souls.

Nehemiah's task was to rebuild the walls of Jerusalem. Enemies of God told him to shut down and consult with them. He replied, *"I am doing a great work, so that I cannot come down: why should the work cease, whilst I leave it, and come down to you?"*[109] I like that! I like his estimate of his work!

---

[107] 1 Kings 21:3; read the entire chapter. *Pastors!* Naboth was murdered for not surrendering to Jezebel. You may be arrested, imprisoned, smeared, vilified and ridiculed. So what? **Do not fear man. Fear God!**
[108] Luke 19:13
[109] Nehemiah 6:3

One greater than Nehemiah has given us our task.

"Preach the Gospel to every creature!"[110]

We have a great work to do, and the urgency and priority of our work ought to move us to "get to getting" no matter who protests or points accusatory fingers. Jesus did not call us to be idle. He did not anoint us to be silent. He did not baptize us in the Holy Spirit so we could hide in a corner until He snatches us up to heaven. He did not give us "the mind of Christ" so we could be embroiled in speculations over the exact date of His return. Jesus is saying to us what He has always said: PREACH THE GOSPEL TO EVERY CREATURE! This divine imperative is still in force and lays squarely on you and on me, and it is tied directly to Jesus' return. Jesus said,

> *"This Gospel of the Kingdom shall be preached in all the world for a witness unto all nations; and then shall the end come."*[111]

Instead of wondering "how close we are to the end," we must go all out to win others to Christ! We miss the mark searching for a "new" word, as if the old one is worn out. The Great Commission is our "now" word, and it is as new in this now moment as it was when it was first spoken by Jesus! What we need is "now" obedience! What we need is "now" faith—faith that America will be saved. *America will be saved* is a prophecy. But it is more than that. *America will be saved* is a rallying cry. *America will be saved* is a call to action. It is a call for you to burn with the fire of God until everyone around you catches fire. You can, by the grace of God, spread the fire of God to thousands.

When thousands of believers catch fire—burning with the love of God and the faith of God—they become uncontainable.

156

---

[110] Mark 16:15
[111] Matthew 24:14

When the thousands become millions, they become unstoppable.

When the millions become billions, they become unconquerable and: Jesus returns!

AFRICA, NOW AMERICA!

The following song was a favorite of Reinhard Bonnke; he first sang it with the words, "Africa shall be saved!"[112]

If you believe and I believe, and we together pray:
The Holy Spirit will come down: America will be saved!
America will be saved! America will be saved!
The Holy Spirit will come down: America will be saved!

If you will fast and I will fast, and we humble ourselves:
Fresh wind from heav'n will surely blow: America will be saved!
America will be saved! America will be saved!
Fresh wind from heav'n will surely blow: America will be saved!

If you live clean and I live clean, and we seek God's face:
His fire will flare, His arm He'll bare: America will be saved!
America will be saved! America will be saved!
His fire will flare, His arm He'll bare: America will be saved!

If you will go and I will go, and we fearlessly preach:
The power of God will be released: America will be saved!
America will be saved! America will be saved!
The power of God will be released: America will be saved!

America's *PASTORS* must lead the way—and they must lead by example. [I address these concluding words to *Pastors*.]

157

---

[112] I added the second, third and fourth verses; to hear the song, see Bonnke's Memorial Service on YouTube.

Pastors! The transformation of America begins with Y-O-U!!!

As Pastors go, believers go. As believers go, churches go. As churches go, the nation goes.

God works in a nation through the people of that nation, and His work begins with the spiritual leadership: with Pastors.

Jesus wants every Pastor to be on fire. Jesus loved the lukewarm church at Laodicea and gave them a promise:

> **"To him that overcomes** *lukewarmness by the power of My grace and burns hot for My glory* **will I grant to sit with Me in My throne:** *so that he can exercise authority over demons that would wreck his nation,* **even as I also overcame** *every temptation to be less than what I was called to be and do,* **and am set down with My Father in His throne."**[113]

The greatest need of America is for every Pastor to be an unquenchable torch of truth, by almighty grace fully obeying God's moral law of love and fearlessly preaching the Gospel of our Lord Jesus Christ!

Pastors! Jesus was full of grace and truth. He was not just full of grace. True grace harmonizes with holiness! Do not pervert the grace of God into a license to commit immorality! That is to deny our Lord Jesus Christ!!! Read *Jude! Jude* is a bold warning from the Holy Spirit: *Do not pervert the grace of God into moral anarchy! False grace will put your fire out and have you accept what God condemns. True grace will make you a burning torch, purifying the very atmosphere of your church and your city. True grace will give you a backbone as well as the bravery and boldness to speak up on the great moral issues of our day.*

---

[113] Revelation 3:21

To be silent when atheistic bullies are trying to take down our nation like Goliath of old, is reprehensible cowardice. Now is not the time for you to be silent or "politically correct." *Rise up and run to the battle, in Jesus' Name!* Haven't you figured out that the real agenda of the devil behind the COVID-19 façade is to shut down churches and to silence preachers? By what demonic wisdom do you readily comply with unconstitutional, unscriptural and ungodly orders to close your doors or limit who may attend? *How dare you!* OPEN YOUR CHURCHES, IN THE MIGHTY NAME OF JESUS!

Pastors! Learn America's history! It was America's *Pastors and preachers* who led the First Great Awakening and who inspired Americans to fight for their independence. We must have another Great Awakening now ... or America will be lost! We must press past what is comfortable and push ourselves beyond the normal. Like Queen Esther, you have been put in your place of leadership "for such a time as this." To have influence with God and man, as you do, and not use it, is criminal. Your leadership is crucial! May you stop the devil from killing America's morals, stealing America's money and destroying America's mission! May the Spirit of God come on you mightily so that, like Samson of old, you tear that devouring lion into pieces! *You can't let the devil win!* Jesus said that the violent take the kingdom of heaven by force: they perceive its value and they pursue it with passionate force until they possess it. Jesus told us that when we pray, what things soever we desire, we are to believe that we TAKE them as our own with a grip that cannot be shaken off, and we shall have them."[114] "What things soever" is broad enough to include Great Awakening in America.

Take Great Awakening by force: by obeying the Holy Spirit, by fasting, by passionate praying, by clean living, by the authoritative command of faith, by unflagging zeal in soulwinning, and most of all, by fiery preaching!!!

---

[114] Matthew 11:12; Mark 11:24

God gave Abraham an unusual promise: *"thy seed shall possess the gate of his enemies."*[115] *Gates* signify the power centers of society. It is the unique destiny of those who have the *uncommon sense* to stay *under God* to control what goes on in the gates. *That's you!* You have the *uncommon faith* of Abraham as well as his *uncommon love* for God.

Pastors! Run all-out with the God-given prophecy that America will be saved! Fearlessly add your agreement.

With *uncommon faith*, call down the fire of God in your church! Either our churches will burn with the fire of God—or our cities will burn. Which do you think the devil wants?

The Gospel is truth on fire. Our Lord Jesus is pleased with hot— therefore, may you be *uncommonly hot* by His almighty grace! May you live clean and live close to God, so that, with clear conscience, you can boldly lead the way! May the Holy Spirit stir in your soul and broaden your vision until all you see is a blood-washed America! God wants the world. God wants America. Step up to God's big vision! Motivate and mobilize God's people, striving with His might to make sure that every believer in your congregation is infused with *uncommon sense*, burns with *uncommon fire* for the Lord Jesus Christ, and works with *uncommon energy* toward making a Great Awakening come to America. Intentionally join with other pastors in your city in impassioned intercession and enthusiastic evangelism, until the Jesus-Movement is the talk of your town. Don't stop there; take it to a higher level: band together with Pastors throughout your state until your state is aflame for the glory of God. Then, we will witness the fulfillment of prophecy:

America will be saved!!!

160

---

[115] Genesis 22:17

The Declaration
of Independence

When, in the course of human events, it becomes necessary for one people to dissolve the political bands which have connected them with another, and to assume, among the powers of the earth, the separate and equal station to which the laws of nature and of nature's God entitle them, a decent respect to the opinions of mankind requires that they should declare the causes which impel them to the separation.

We hold these truths to be self-evident, that all men are created equal, that they are endowed by their Creator with certain unalienable rights, that among these are life, liberty, and the pursuit of happiness. That, to secure these rights, governments are instituted among men, deriving their just powers from the consent of the governed. That, whenever any form of government becomes destructive of these ends, it is the right of the people to alter or to abolish it, and to institute new government, laying its foundation on such principles, and organizing its powers in such form, as to them shall seem most likely to effect their safety and happiness.

Prudence, indeed, will dictate that governments long established should not be changed for light and transient causes; and, accordingly, all experience has shown, that mankind are more disposed to suffer, while evils are sufferable, than to right themselves by abolishing the forms to which they are accustomed.

But, when a long train of abuses and usurpations, pursuing invariably the same object, evinces a design to reduce them under absolute despotism, it is their right, it is their duty, to throw off such government, and to provide new guards for their future security. Such has been the patient sufferance of these colonies; and such is now the necessity which constrains them to alter their former systems of government. **The history of the present King of Great Britain is a history of repeated injuries and usurpations, all having in direct object the establishment of an absolute tyranny over these states.** To prove this, let facts be submitted to a candid world.

He has refused his assent to laws the most wholesome and necessary for the public good.

He has forbidden his governors to pass laws of immediate and pressing importance, unless suspended in their operation till his assent should be obtained; and when so suspended, he has utterly neglected to attend to them.

He has refused to pass other laws for the accommodation of large districts of people, unless those people would relinquish the right of representation in the legislature; a right inestimable to them and formidable to tyrants only.

He has called together legislative bodies at places unusual, uncomfortable, and distant from the depository of their public records, for the sole purpose of fatiguing them into compliance with his measures.

He has dissolved representative houses repeatedly, for opposing, with manly firmness, his invasions on the rights of the people.

He has refused for a long time, after such dissolutions, to cause others to be elected; whereby the legislative powers, incapable of annihilation, have returned to the people at large for their exercise; the state remaining in the meantime exposed to all the dangers of invasion from without, and convulsions within.

He has endeavored to prevent the population of these states; for that purpose obstructing the laws for naturalization of foreigners; refusing to pass others to encourage their migrations hither, and raising the conditions of new appropriations of lands.

He has obstructed the administration of justice, by refusing his assent to laws for establishing judiciary powers.

He has made judges dependent on his will alone, for the tenure of their offices, and the amount and payment of their salaries.

He has erected a multitude of new offices, and sent hither swarms of officers to harass our people, and eat out their substance.

He has kept among us, in times of peace, standing armies, without the consent of our legislatures.

He has affected to render the military independent of and superior to the civil power.

He has combined with others to subject us to a jurisdiction foreign to our constitution, and unacknowledged by our laws; giving his assent to their acts of pretended legislation:

For quartering large bodies of armed troops among us;

For protecting them, by a mock trial, from punishment for any murders which they should commit on the inhabitants of these states;

For cutting off our trade with all parts of the world;

For imposing taxes on us without our consent;

For depriving us, in many cases, of the benefits of trial by jury;

For transporting us beyond seas to be tried for pretended offenses;

For abolishing the free system of English laws in a neighboring province, establishing therein an arbitrary government, and enlarging its boundaries, so as to render it at once an example and fit instrument for introducing the same absolute rule into these colonies;

For taking away our charters, abolishing our most valuable laws, and altering fundamentally the forms of our governments;

For suspending our own legislatures, and declaring themselves invested with power to legislate for us in all cases whatsoever.

He has abdicated government here, by declaring us out of his protection, and waging war against us.

He has plundered our seas, ravaged our coasts, burnt our towns, and destroyed the lives of our people.

He is at this time transporting large armies of foreign mercenaries to complete the works of death, desolation, and tyranny, already begun with circumstances of cruelty and perfidy scarcely paralleled in the most barbarous ages, and totally unworthy the head of a civilized nation.

He has constrained our fellow citizens, taken captive on the high seas, to bear arms against their country, to become the executioners of their friends and brethren, or to fall themselves by their hands.

He has excited domestic insurrections amongst us, and has endeavored to bring on the inhabitants of our frontiers, the merciless Indian savages, whose known rule of warfare is an undistinguished destruction of all ages, sexes, and conditions.

In every stage of these oppressions, we have petitioned for redress, in the most humble terms. Our repeated petitions have been answered only by repeated injury. **A prince, whose character is thus marked by every act which may define a tyrant, is unfit to be the ruler of a free people.**

Nor have we been wanting in attentions to our British brethren. We have warned them from time to time of attempts by their legislature to extend an unwarrantable jurisdiction over us. We have reminded them of the circumstances of our emigration and settlement here. We have appealed to their native justice and magnanimity, and we have conjured them by the ties of our common kindred, to disavow these usurpations, which would inevitably interrupt our connections and correspondence. They too have been deaf to the voice of justice and of consanguinity. We must, therefore acquiesce in the necessity, which denounces our separation, and hold them, as we hold the rest of mankind, enemies in war, in peace friends.

We, therefore, the representatives of the United States pf America, in General Congress assembled, **appealing to the Supreme Judge of the world for the rectitude of our intentions,** *do, in the name, and by authority of the good people of these colonies, solemnly publish and declare, that these United Colonies are, and of right ought to be free and independent states; that they are absolved from all allegiance to the British Crown, and that all political connection between them and the state of Great Britain is and ought to be totally dissolved; and that, as free and independent states, they have full power to levy war, conclude peace, contract alliances, establish commerce, and to do all other acts and things which independent states may of right do. And for the support of this declaration,* **with a firm reliance on the protection of Divine Providence,** *we mutually pledge to each other our lives, our fortunes, and our sacred honor.*

Not long from now, on July 4, 2026, we will celebrate the 250th anniversary of the *Declaration of Independence!* May we so take to heart the magnitude of our responsibility under God that on that day, we will celebrate what still gloriously is, and not mourn over what once was.

Letter Of Samuel Adams

Samuel Adams to James Warren
Philadelphia, February 12th, 1779

My dear Sir ...

A general dissolution of principles and manners will more surely overthrow the liberties of America than the whole force of the Common Enemy.

WHILE THE PEOPLE ARE VIRTUOUS THEY CANNOT BE SUBDUED; BUT WHEN ONCE THEY LOSE THEIR VIRTUE THEY WILL BE READY TO SURRENDER THEIR LIBERTIES TO THE FIRST EXTERNAL OR INTERNAL INVADER ...

I do verily believe ... that **the principles and manners of New England produced that Spirit which finally has established the Independence of America; and nothing but opposite principles and manners can overthrow it. ... If virtue and knowledge are diffused among the People, they will never be enslaved. This will be their great security. Virtue and knowledge will forever be an even balance for powers and riches.** I hope our Countrymen will never depart from the principles and maxims which have been handed down to us from our wise forefathers. This greatly depends upon the example of men of character and influence of the present day. This is a subject my heart is much set upon. But I fear I have wearied your patience.

I will conclude with my most ardent prayer that our last days may be our best days and our last works our best works.

AMERICA! AMERICA!

V1. O beautiful for Bible Truth
The Rock on which we stand
Whose wisdom formed our nation's youth
And made us freedom's land.
America! America!
The Bible is divine.
Your soul to feed, the Bible read.
God's Word is your lifeline!

V2. O beautiful for preachers brave
Who spread the Gospel light;
Who by their fire a nation save
From atheistic blight!
America! America!
Come under God and pray!
Forsake your pride—be on God's side:
His Word gladly obey!

V3. O beautiful for churches strong
Who boldly lead the way,
Who by their love show right from wrong
And bring a brighter day!
America! America!
Choose life for one and all!
Choose love, not hate! It's not too late:
Answer God's higher call!

I HAVE A SPINE

"You can make me feel alone,
remove me far from my home:
but you can't take me away from my God."
Daniel had a spine.

"You can change my nation,
alter my location:
but you can't change my eternal destination."
Daniel had a spine.

"You can change my language—that's true;
but there's one thing you cannot do:
you can't change my first love."
Daniel had a spine.

"You can change my name
as if I would bring your god fame:
but you can't change my heart's allegiance."
Daniel had a spine.

"You can even castrate me
rob me of my masculinity:
but you can't change my core identity."
Daniel had a spine.

"You can make me a slave,
threaten me with the grave:
but you can't order me not to pray."
Daniel had a spine.

"You can't command the longing of my heart,
control the focus of my soul,
or corrupt my morals."
Daniel had a spine.

"You can't desensitize my conscience,
determine my outlook on life,
or dictate the intensity of my prayer."
Daniel had a spine.

"You can put chains on my hands and feet,
but you can't put chains on my soul:
you can't ever reach that!"
Daniel had a spine.

"You can change my language, my country,
my name and even parts of my body:
but you can't change my God!"
Daniel had a spine.

Have you forgotten?
Our government derives its just powers
from the consent of the governed.
Hear this!
To tyrannical, ever-expanding, over-reaching government
I DO NOT CONSENT.
I HAVE A SPINE.

To replacing our *Declaration* and our Constitution
with an oligarchy of tyrants and their draconian rules
I DO NOT CONSENT.
I HAVE A SPINE.

They may monitor where I go
and surveil what I do:
but they can't track my spirit soaring up to God!
They can't change my Lord and my God: JESUS!
They may try to steal my vote and silence my voice,
but they can't ever change me:
I HAVE A SPINE.

AMERICA WILL BE SAVED!

An evil king came to the dying prophet, crying tears:
Tears of self-pity, for he was trapped in his fears
Knowing that when the prophet passed on
The nation's only connection to God would be gone
But, his honoring the prophet, late though it was
Gave God the chance to create a miracle-buzz
The king's enemies would be beaten—to what degree?
It was up to the king: not God's sovereignty.

The king, armed with bow and arrow, gave attention
"Shoot through the open window!" was the direction
"The arrow of the Lord's deliverance" was the explanation
"Now, strike the ground!" was the prophet's command
The king tapped the ground three times and stopped
The prophet, furious, was in shock:
The king's nonchalance at this God-given opportunity
Meant he would have only partial victory.

America will be saved! What a tremendous prophecy!
Do you believe it, but query: To what degree?
God is faithful, tis true: His promise He will keep:
But it is our duty to wake up, and not remain asleep!
Our faith and our fire, our passion and our purity:
These factors, with their unique potency,
Determine the fulfillment of the prophecy.
God has left it up to us, in His majestic sovereignty!

(read 2 Kings 13:14-19,25)

Real Freedom

Four freedoms, now under attack:
Freedom of worship, freedom from lack
Freedom of speech, freedom from fear
All four, we Americans hold dear.
A fifth freedom is the root of all the rest:
Freedom from sin is the first and the best
Such a gift no mortal can give
Only He who forever lives!

Jesus alone gives real liberty
Freedom is His gift, with prosperity
He grants salvation and security
He bestows life and tranquility.
Jesus alone breaks sin's bitter bondage
And gladly gives us a better heritage.
Freedom from sin is the heart foundation,
The indispensable bedrock of a free nation.

A counterfeit is a fake and a fraud
Perpetrated on those who forget God.
Freedom to sin without punishment?
A mirage! And to stupidity, a monument.
This "freedom" brings invisible chains
Stripping a nation of all its gains.
This "freedom" will cause America to crumble
The key issue is: will you be humble?

Humble enough to receive Jesus as Lord?
Humble enough to obey His holy Word?
Or will you be content with lovely illusion?
Will you be swept away by strong delusion?
As for me, to Jesus I cry:
Visit us now, my Lord, or America will die!

Eternal Truth

"Why do the heathen rage *against God*,
and the people imagine a vain thing *that will come to nothing?*
The kings of the earth set themselves,
and the rulers take counsel together, *scheming*
against the LORD, and against His Anointed, saying,
'Let us break their bands asunder,
and cast away their cords from us'"
*thus despising and discarding His holy commandments
that bring us real freedom.
What is God's response? Is He all shook up? No way!*
"He that sitteth in the heavens shall laugh:
the LORD shall have them in derision.
Then shall He speak unto them in His wrath,
and vex them in His sore displeasure.
Yet have I set My king upon My holy hill of Zion.
I will declare the decree:
the LORD hath said unto Me,
Thou art My Son; this day have I begotten Thee.
Ask of Me, and I shall give Thee
the heathen for Thine inheritance,
and the uttermost parts of the earth for Thy possession.
Thou shalt break them with a rod of iron;
Thou shalt dash them in pieces like a potter's vessel.
Be wise now therefore, O ye *rebellious* kings:
be instructed, ye judges of the earth. *Forsake your madness!*
Serve the LORD with fear, and rejoice with trembling.
KISS THE SON—*this is your duty, under God*—
lest He be angry, and ye perish from the way,
when His wrath is kindled but a little.
Blessed are all they that put their trust in Him."
—Psalm 2 *[author's comments in italics]*
"By the word of the LORD were the heavens made ... He spoke,
and it was done; He commanded, and it stood fast.

The LORD brings the counsel of the heathen to nothing:
He makes the sinister schemes of the wicked of none effect.
The counsel of the LORD stands forever,
the thoughts of His heart to all generations.
Blessed is the nation whose God is the LORD."
—Psalm 33:6,9-12

"Fret not thyself because of evildoers, neither be thou envious
against the workers of iniquity ... For evildoers shall be cut off:
but those that wait upon the LORD, they shall inherit the earth.
For yet a little while, and the wicked shall not be;
they will be gone with wind; yea, thou shalt diligently consider his
place, and it shall not be ... The wicked plots against the just,
and gnashes upon him with his teeth. The LORD shall laugh at him:
for He sees that his day is coming. The wicked have drawn out the
sword, and have bent their bow, to cast down the poor and needy,
and to slay such as be of upright conversation.
Their sword shall enter into their own heart,
and their bows shall be broken."
—Psalm 37:1,9,10,12-15 *[author's comments in italics]*

"Fear ye not Me? saith the LORD:
will ye not tremble at My presence,
which have placed the sand for the bound of the sea
by a perpetual decree, that it cannot pass it:
and though the waves thereof toss themselves,
yet can they not prevail;
though they roar, yet can they not pass over it?"
—Jeremiah 5:22

"I will build My church,
and the gates of hell shall not prevail against it."
—the Lord Jesus Christ, Matthew 16:18

CPSIA information can be obtained
at www.ICGtesting.com
Printed in the USA
FSHW021837090321
79300FS